PANZER ELITE

PANZER ELITE

THE STORY OF NAZI GERMANY'S CRACK
GROSSDEUTSCHLAND CORPS

James Lucas

TEMPUS

First published 2000

PUBLISHED IN THE UNITED KINGDOM BY:

Tempus Publishing Ltd
The Mill, Brimscombe Port
Stroud, Gloucestershire GL5 2QG

PUBLISHED IN THE UNITED STATES OF AMERICA BY:

Arcadia Publishing Inc.
A division of Tempus Publishing Inc.
2 Cumberland Street
Charleston, SC 29401
1-888-313-2665

Tempus books are available in France, Germany and Belgium
from the following addresses:

Tempus Publishing Group	Tempus Publishing Group	Tempus Publishing Group
21 Avenue de la République	Gustav-Adolf-Straße 3	Place de L'Alma 4/5
37300 Joué-lès-Tours	99084 Erfurt	1200 Brussels
FRANCE	GERMANY	BELGIUM

British Library Cataloguing in Publication Data.
A catalogue record for this book is available from the British Library.

ISBN 0 7524 2020 8

Typesetting and origination by Tempus Publishing.
PRINTED AND BOUND IN GREAT BRITAIN

.

Contents

Acknowledgements

To all those who have helped in the preparation of this book go my sincerest and most grateful thanks. To Traude, my wife, to Barbara Shaw and to Mary Harris who typed the manuscript; to Brian Leigh Davis and to Janusz Piekalkiewicz for permission to quote from their books and who supplied me with photographs. To Matthew Cooper, Philip Reed and Terry Charman for their invaluable advice. I am grateful also to the numerous ex-soldiers and Old Comrades Associations upon whose memories of battle and campaigning, letters and diaries I have drawn.

Foreword

The crowd which had gathered near the memorial a short distance from the Brandenburger Tor on a sunny Sunday morning in 1939 craned forward expectantly as the far-off sound of martial music was heard above the noise of the Berlin traffic. It was just a few minutes before midday. Then, as the seconds ticked away, the music, louder now, carried with it a rhythmic undertone: the sound of jackboots crashing down in unison upon stone. The bass drummer of the still unseen band beat out a few successive and rapid beats to change the tune of the march so that punctually at noon, as the first files of the band passed under the great, granite arch, the opening bars of *Deutschland über Alles* thundered upwards to be reflected back from the roof of the Brandenburger Tor. They were changing the guard in Berlin and a full detachment of troops with its regimental band was carrying out the ceremony. The Infantry Regiment Grossdeutschland – newly named out of the old Wach Regiment Berlin – was demonstrating to the world that the spirit of Prussian Germany had been revived; if indeed it had ever died in the few years which had passed from the demise of the Empire to the birth of National Socialist Germany's Third Reich.

Just under six years later, shortly before midnight on 1 May 1945 the exhausted survivors of the Wach Regiment Grossdeutschland lay under shell and mortar fire in Berlin's Kastanien Allee, grouping themselves to break through the ring of Soviet soldiers which surrounded the dying capital and hoping to reach the west. Berlin was going down in a mass of flames and explosions as the Soviet Army made the last great assault to finish that bitter war which the Third Reich had begun. Berlin surrendered two days later and as the fighting died down, there died with it the political dream of a Greater Germany. Hitler's concept of a Grossdeutschland perished in the misery of a lost war.

At a number of other places in those sectors which had once formed the Eastern and

Western Fronts, men whose tunics bore cuff bands showing their allegiance to one or the other of the units comprising the Grossdeutschland organisation were marching into the years of captivity which awaited some of them. The Soviets showed no mercy to the men of Grossdeutschland for the titles on their sleeve proclaimed the privileged place which they had held in the army of the Third Reich and this distinction had to be paid for even if it had only been the prerogative of those units to be in action almost continually and always at posts of the maximum danger.

The Grossdeutschland units were crack formations upon whose ability the German front in the east depended. From 1940 to 1945 theirs is a story of almost continuous front line service: the men deeply aware of the mystical bond that linked them and the nation whose name they bore; and their officers, the selected products of the finest military training available at that time, reflecting in their competency the maxim of von Seeckt, the father of the army of the Third Reich, *'Mehr sein als Schein'* ('Be more than you appear to be').

This, then, is the history of an elite unit whose life span was little more than two thousand days but which, in that short space of time, won for itself a reputation for reliability and devotion to duty which is imperishable.

Introduction

Extreme political movements have ideologies born out of years of struggle; great times find their men of destiny and world wars produce military commanders and units whose outstanding ability ensures that their reputations live beyond the mere years of their existence. The political movement in Germany produced Adolf Hitler in whose mind burned the dream of Grossdeutschland and this idea on a military level was bestowed, initially, upon a German infantry regiment chosen to carry out ceremonial duties.

The English language translation 'Greater Germany' does not, indeed cannot, convey the emotive power which lies within the single German noun Grossdeutschland. Bismarck's ideal of a completely united Germany was not to be realised until the years of the short-lived Third Reich, by which time the Iron Chancellor's ambition was considered too limited. What the leaders of National Socialist Germany dreamed of was not his unification of the German kingdoms, states and provinces into a single nation but nothing less than the return of all Germans living outside the borders of the Fatherland. 'Heim in's Reich' ('The return home to Germany') was the new rallying cry.

To achieve this national dream those provinces which had belonged to her, and which, as the Germans saw it, had been torn from her as a result of Versailles and other treaties forced upon a prostrate and defeated nation by the victorious Allies after the First World War, would be reunited with the Fatherland and those *Volksdeutsche,* the men and women in German colonies dispersed across Europe, together with those others who had been forced to emigrate for political reasons of persecution or through unemployment, would all return home. To German emotions the concept of Grossdeutschland was not an abstract theory but an appeal as potent as is Zionism to Jewish sentiments.

Prominent among the myths of the Second World War is the legend that of all the German military forces only the Waffen SS had the aura of invincibility, but this is a claim which does not bear close and critical scrutiny. It is true that from the great mass of divisions and corps which made up the German Army, units of the SS did stand distinct and clear, but they were not alone. Head and shoulders above the rest were Army units – corps as well as divisions. The Afrika Korps, Rommel's 7th Panzer Division in the French campaign of 1940 and 5th Gebirgsjager Division all won for themselves reputations second to none, but over them all towers the name of the Grossdeutschland formations, the *primus inter pares* of all that select company whose names are imperishable in the military history of the German Army in the Second World War.

The astonishing, dramatic growth of the German Army in the years of the Third Reich; a carefully manipulated balance between pragmatism and tradition allowed elite units to expand and to rise in strength. In the case of the Wach Regiment Berlin which then became the Infantry Regiment Grossdeutschland this was an increase to that of a Panzer Corps whose establishment included one of Germany's least known but most experienced units, Brandenburg. Also of, but not in, the Grossdeutschland establishment and descended from the Wach Regiment Berlin were other elite formations, including the Führer Begleit and the Führer Grenadier Divisions.

This, then, is the story of a regiment which rose to become a corps and which produced a number of progeny in the course of its military life. Regimental histories are warm and vital records of individuals or small groups used tactically. Divisional or corps histories recount strategic movements and are less closely detailed.

This account records in the first campaigns the small unit feeling and this I have attempted to maintain also for those years during which Grossdeutschland rose to become a Panzer Corps. In order that the narrative flow is not interrupted where new Grossdeutschland formations are born no detailed description of them will be given at that point in the text. The biographical details of the most important units in the Grossdeutschland establishment will be found in the chapters following the main story.

One
The Genesis of the Infantry Regiment Grossdeutschland

'In our proud name we incorporate the Armed Forces of Greater Germany… Just as we march at the head of every parade so should we, if the need ever arise, be the first to storm into battle.'
The Regimental Commander, June 1939

The armistice which brought to an end the First World War produced the collapse of the Imperial German Army and under the terms of the Treaty of Versailles the strength of the new Army of the Republic was limited to 100,000 men whose task it was to maintain law and order within the national borders.

In the immediate post-war period attempts to invade and to occupy German territory were frustrated by German ex-Servicemen organised into Freikorps units. There was, however, a greater danger from within Germany, of coups d'etat from one or other of the two extreme political wings. To defeat any attempts to overthrow the government strong and reliable forces were needed within the Reich capital city of Berlin until at last the danger of revolution receded. A permanent military body was, however, still needed in Berlin, if for no other reason than to carry out ceremonial parades and guard duties. The first, formally organised body raised to carry out such duties, the Wach Regiment Berlin, was formed and disbanded during 1921. A new unit with the vague name *Kommando der Wachtruppe* (Headquarters Guard Troop) was then raised and remained practically unaltered in composition, establishment or duties, for the next thirteen years.

During this time the *Kommando der Wachtruppe* provided the people of Berlin with a daily military spectacle. On four days of the week there was a simple, standard guard changing but on Sunday, Tuesday and Thursday a full Guard, including the regimental band, left the Moabit barracks and passed through the Brandenburg Gate en route to the War Memorial.

In 1934 there came a change of title to *Wachtruppe Berlin* (Berlin Guard Troops) and within two years an increase in establishment from seven to eight companies and the raising of an headquarters company to administer the unit. In June 1937 the unit name was changed, once again, and it was now known as *Wach Regiment Berlin* (The Berlin Guard Regiment).

From the very earliest days of its existence it had been the practice to draw the men needed for the Guard detachment by whole companies – one from each of the seven divisions into which the original republican Army had been organised. Each company served a three-month term of secondment to the Guard and were then returned to their parent unit. Under Hitler the Army had increased in number and was now, once again, organised in Army Corps but the selection of men for the Guard remained the same. Then came a radical change in policy and men were no longer obtained by companies. Instead individual soldiers or small groups from a regiment were specially selected and seconded to the Guard on a half-yearly posting. Officers and NCOs selected for that duty were on a year's secondment.

In order that a cadre of fully trained senior ranks was available at all times only 50% of the total number was returned to unit at any one time and to ensure continuity a depot company was also raised.

The main of the Wach Regiment was now heavily committed to the guard duties for which it had been raised but Hitler's Germany was growing in size and in importance. It was now no longer Deutschland but was on the way to becoming Grossdeutschland; firstly as a result of the re-occupation of the Rhineland, in 1935, then by the annexation of Austria in March 1938 and finally through the occupation of the Sudetenland in September of the same year. For the Führer to see his new Grossdeutschland it was necessary that he move outside the former national boundaries and for such journeys a twenty-man detachment of the Wach Regiment Berlin was on permanent standby ready to accompany and to protect Hitler throughout the trips. This escort unit, the Führer Begleit, will be dealt with in the following pages.

Germany's growing political importance was reflected in the increased number of State visits and conferences which took place, for each of which a guard of honour was found by the Wach Regiment. Drill standards of astonishing precision produced the perfect military spectacle. Drill and the barrack square dominated the life of the men of the Wach Regiment and Saturday morning was taken up with a vast regimental parade at which every available company and both bands were present. Long hours were spent perfecting arms drill positions; there were marches past in line and in column and the whole time there came the noise of the crashing of studded boots on stone as the detachments practised the most famous of all military marches – the goose step.

The early days of the Infantry Regiment Grossdeutschland.

In the first week of April 1939 Hitler, the Supreme Commander of the Armed Forces and German Chancellor, ordered the regiment to be reorganised during the coming autumn and for it to receive a new name Infantry Regiment Grossdeutschland. The formal date of birth of the new unit was 14 June 1939. This reorganisation produced a fundamental change in that as a permanently based regiment it would no longer have to rely upon drafts of seconded men but, instead, would recruit volunteers which the regiment would itself train. To comply with its proud title this was to be no locally raised unit, restricted territorially to men of a particular province. Instead recruits would be accepted from all over Germany and would thus give to the new regiment the best of the nation's manhood. Each would be a volunteer, would be not merely physically but mentally and morally fit to serve in the premier infantry regiment of the German Army and would embody the ideal of the German warrior spirit.

In keeping with the spirit of the new formation and to establish its elite character a special uniform was designed. A major preoccupation of Hitler's regime was to demonstrate its links with Germany's great soldierly traditions and many of the features of the new uniform proposed for the Infantry Regiment Grossdeutschland, reflected those links which the National Socialist Government wished to emphasise. A full description of the tunic and the overcoat will be found in other pages of this book.

It was now the high summer of 1939. With the rump of Czechoslovakia occupied by the Germans, political pressure was applied to Poland and crises developed as Hitler made threats against that nation. Rumours of war were in the air and it was no time for professional soldiers to be considering the details of piping on a tunic or the design of cuff lace. In the event the new uniform was never issued and even supplies of a green and silver cuff band were insufficient for general distribution. With only a monogram on their shoulder straps to mark their exclusiveness the men of the Infantry Regiment Grossdeutschland continued their public duties outwardly applying themselves to the business of guard mounting and ceremonial parades, while concentrating upon building up the unit to a state of readiness for war.

The outbreak of hostilities in September 1939 was paradoxically a relief from the terrible tension which had built up. The political decision to take up arms had been made and the professional soldiers of the Grossdeutschland regiment waited with firm resolve and high hearts for the call to action. Their spirits were dashed with the announcement that the regiment would not be marching out with the rest of the army to take part in the campaign against Poland. This was an unpopular order and there were many who felt that as professionals they should have been among the first to go; they felt that they had been deprived of the chance to fight for the nation whose name they bore.

Two

Infantry Regiment Grossdeutschland's First Campaign: France, 1940

Although the regiment had been denied the opportunity to fight in the successful campaign against Poland, Germany's two principal enemies, France and Great Britain still remained in the field and as long as they did so the officers and men of the Infantry Regiment Grossdeutschland would have the opportunity to serve their country. In anticipation of future campaigns the features of the succeeding months were reorganisations and accretions of strength, for experience gained from the Polish campaign had convinced the German High Command of the need to expand the motorised infantry arm of service. Accordingly the regiment increased its establishment in vehicles, artillery and engineers. Slowly but steadily Grossdeutschland prepared itself for the time when it would take part in the war.

Adolf Hitler, having taken upon himself the task of making all major military decisions, ordered in October 1939 that a campaign be opened on the Western Front without delay but, persuaded by the General Staff that such a move was premature, reluctantly postponed it; the first of the twenty or more such postponements which were to come before, in the spring of 1940, the German armies struck across the frontier and into the Netherlands, Belgium and northern France. The wartime role of an independent regiment, even with a name as distinctive as that of Grossdeutschland, must be an unsatisfactory one for it must serve in a subordinate role without a real opportunity to

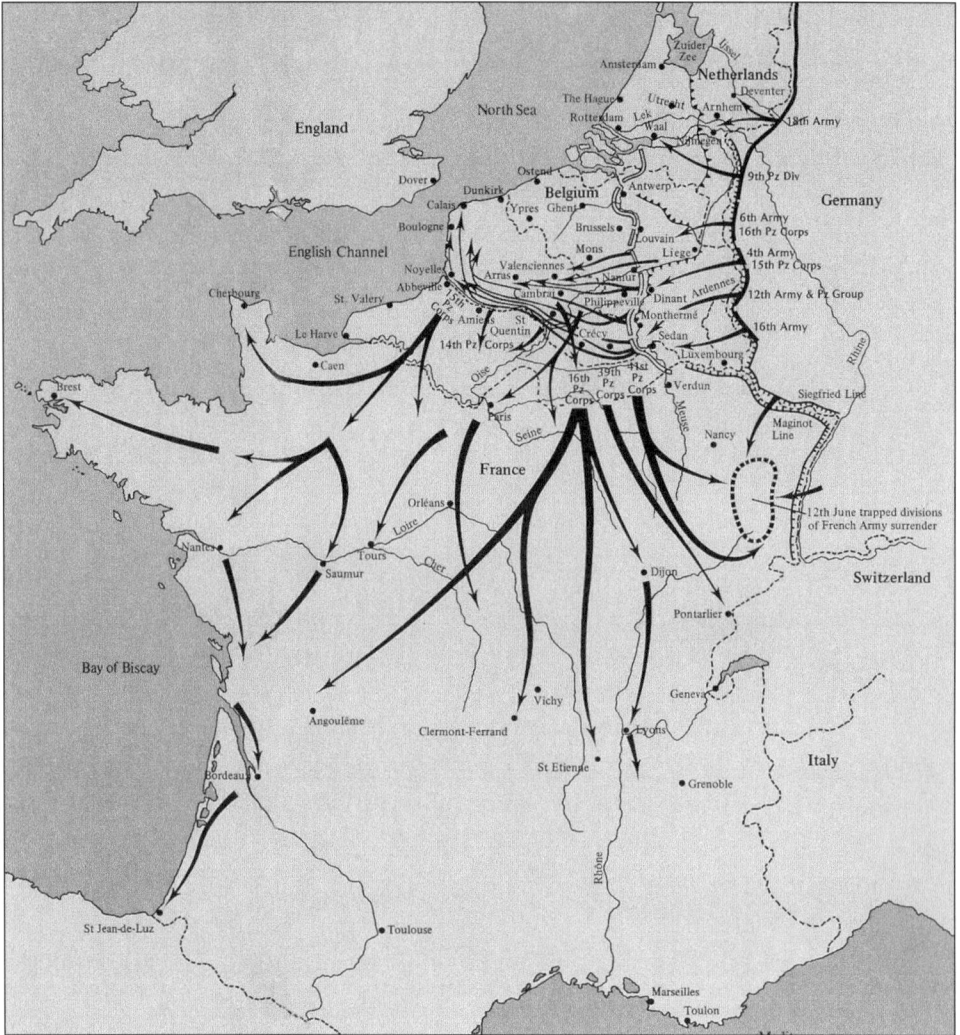

Invasion of Belgium and France.

demonstrate its true abilities. Being thus subordinate it is right to touch only lightly upon the regiment's experiences in both the French and the first Soviet campaigns. Only brief details of these will be given, illustrated with fuller information where this will demonstrate the type of warfare in which the unit was involved.

This is not to deny the regiment's capability for, during the campaign in the west, it undertook the first of those spearhead unit operations which were to lead it, eventually, into the role of the Führer's fire brigade.

The short campaign which smashed the Allied armies and brought the Netherlands, Belgium, France and Luxembourg under German occupation opened on 10 May. The main effort was to be made by Army Group A whose Panzer Group Kleist was to strike through the Ardennes, to drive an armoured wedge into the French armies and then to expand the wedge; speed being the keynote of success. To achieve this certain operations were undertaken which involved great elements of risk. Two of these concerned the Grossdeutschland regiment and are given in detail for they illustrate the spirit of the men of the regiment.

Speed, the vital factor in the military calculation, was nowhere more important than in the first days for it was essential that the western bank of the Meuse be reached without delay. Only when this had been accomplished could the second phase – exploitation and the advance to the sea – be undertaken.

The Infantry Regiment Grossdeutschland was placed in Guderian's Corps, part of the spearhead of Panzer Group Kleist, and for the opening days of the attack the regiment's main effort would be carried out by only two battalions; the 3rd Battalion had been selected for one of the special operations mentioned above. This was to be an air landing behind the Belgian frontier line by 3rd Battalion and code named Operation *Nivi*. But before we go on to describe this let us place ourselves with the main of the regiment and with the men who, aware that an offensive was imminent, were making ready for their baptism of fire.

During the late evening of 9 May 1940, the code signal '*Hindenburg – Gelb* – 10. 05.35' flashed from *Oberkommando der Wehrmacht* (OKW) – the High Command of the Armed Forces – to all major units and was passed by them to their subordinate formations. The campaign in the west was to open at 05.35hr on the following morning. Acting upon that message the regiment moved at 18.00hr towards its form-up line, along roads, paths and bridleways made familiar through weeks of reconnaissance and manoeuvres.

A French observation plane flying high on that cloudless night reported that stretching back for a hundred miles into Germany were the headlights of an army of vehicles heading towards and through the Ardennes and along a vast arc from Wurttemberg to the north of the Netherlands other small groups of German soldiers were moving forward to their start lines. Behind them in Germany, in the darkness just before dawn, squadrons of *Luftwaffe* aircraft were preparing for take-off and the paratroops seated in their swaying gliders were already airborne and en route to their several objectives. The sky began to lighten just before H-hour and in the growing radiance of a perfect early summer dawn the German Army rolled forward and into the opening moves of a new campaign in the west.

While the mass of the Grossdeutschland Regiment was thrusting towards Belgium the men of 3rd Battalion were undertaking Operation *Nivi*. The details given here concerning this daring and unique air landing have been summarised with the permission of the author, from *Fieseler Fi 156 Storch im Zweiten Weltkrieg* by Janusz Piekalkiewicz. I am also indebted to him for permission to use some of the photographs illustrating the operation.

During the preparations for the campaign one of the *Luftwaffe*'s most important tasks was to support von Kleist's panzer troops and to take out the first obstacle in the path of the attacking Panzer divisions, the Belgian frontier defensive post of Bodange near Martelange.

As all the Air Corps, dive bomber formations or para divisions had been detailed for their several tasks for the proposed operation 100 Fieseler Fi 156 were to be used to air land 400 men of Grossdeutschland Infantry Regiment behind the Belgian frontier and were to open the campaign with a top secret special mission which has remained almost unknown until this day. It was to be the greatest and at the same time most demanding operation carried out by these aircraft in the whole of the Second World War.

The Army High Command plan was for Garski's battalion to cut signals and telephone communications; to obstruct the movement of reserves; and by exerting pressure upon the rear of the bunker line around Bodange along the frontier, to capture this and thus to facilitate the advance.

For these purposes two sections were to be formed and were to land in the area of Nives and Witry. The flight in would have to take place in two waves as there was room for only two soldiers in each machine. According to the time-table the second wave was to arrive within two hours of the first.

The main effort was to be made with the southern detachment 'Witry' and this was, therefore, the larger detachment. 'Nives', the northern unit, was a company strong with Pioneer reinforcements while the southern section contained battalion HQ and a company, supported by mortars and other weapons.

Forty-two machines were needed to transport the northern detachment and fifty-six for the southern group. Weight limitations restricted the ammunition carried to a normal load per person and as this would be insufficient, should the groups become involved in heavy fighting, three Ju52s were to air drop ammunition.

The men selected to undertake Operation *Nivi* were chosen during February 1940 and trained in Crailsheim in conditions of the strictest secrecy. At about 14.15hr on 9 May 1940 the battalion received its alarm call and marched, fully motorised, to aerodromes from which the operation would start.

In the final discussions it was agreed that the Stukas would drop bombs on anti-tank/aircraft positions in the area of the landing points and the hamlet of Vaux les Rosieres where there was said to be a Belgian MG Company in position after the first wave of Storks had landed.

Spirits were high as NCOs checked each man's equipment. Each man carried two linen haversacks. In one there were hand grenades and ammunition and in the other special rations.

Take-off was at 05.20hr and punctually at 05.35hr Garski crossed the Luxembourg frontier. We had expected to be fired at as we flew over Perl on the Belgian frontier but there was not a shot. We flew across the Belgian lines, reached the woods and were safe.

The flight had lasted half an hour and we landed exactly between Witry and the little hamlet of Traimont, on a field near the road.

There was nothing following the two Storks which had landed and already had begun to take off again. The field which was covered with a slight mist remained empty. Four men who had landed south of the road came running towards us bringing two machine guns. The colonel ordered the men to block the road. We were ten men inside enemy territory and could expect no reinforcement until 20.00hr.

From the top of a rise which had a good view of the surrounding countryside and a first class field of fire. We discussed what we should do if a battalion of Ardennes Chasseurs should arrive, but everything remained quiet and we sent out a patrol. At 08.00 a lorry arrived with two platoons commanded by Lieutenant Colonel von Harder. Now we were eighty men strong and occupied Traimont as well as the high ground facing west towards Neu Chatell. Two enemy patrols were captured. Then a Belgian military truck was taken.

A Stork sent by the colonel landed at 21.00hr asking for news and as it took off French artillery opened fire upon it. The barrage grew in intensity and tanks began to show themselves. The nearest approached to within 80m. The anti-tank riflemen opened fire and after the second shot flames began to appear and the tank burnt out. The second machine was hit and halted. The other two AFVs managed to escape in a hollow.

Towards midday of the following day a motor cyclist pulled into Traimont and reported that Captain Kruger and the main of the battalion was en route from Leflife, some 8 to 10km south of Witry. The group had been landed at the wrong place.

Garski's group had been fired upon from the high ground south of Witry and the colonel had been about to put in an attack when Kruger's group arrived. At Bodange there was movement and a line of men was seen. Were these friend or foe? Garski gave the order to tie yellow cloths to bayonets and to wave them. In reply to this agreed signal a large swastika flag was displayed from the troops on the high ground. Thus 3rd Battalion linked up with 1st Panzer Division.'

The main of the regiment had, meanwhile, thrust through Luxembourg into Belgium and towards the Meuse along whose line the French High Command planned to hold the German advance for at least eight days.

Army Group A was, however, approaching the river almost at a gallop, intending to 'bounce' it before the French could bolster their shattered troops and reinforce the defence. The risks attendant upon the lack of time to organise the crossing, the absence of back-up units and of heavy artillery were accepted. The Meuse had to be crossed on 13 May. Guderian's Panzer divisions formed line abreast on a front above and below Sedan and to Infantry Regiment Grossdeutschland, who for this operation was to serve with 1st Panzer Division, there was a welcome addition to its strength with the return of its 3rd Battalion.

First hand accounts by those who take part in the battles and who help to make history are always lively and dramatic in their simplicity, for they speak with the authentic voice of the front line soldier. One such account is that by *Oberleutnant* von Coubiere, as he was then, which is summarised here. The full account originally appeared in Guderian's book

Mit den Panzer im Ost und West, and covers the crossing of the Meuse and the capture of the dominating height, Point 247.

> *13 May 1940. Whit Monday. We have a long night march behind us, and now towards midday the sun burns hot and mercilessly. The companies of 2nd Battalion are resting near their camouflaged vehicles sleeping and strengthening themselves for the battle which lies ahead, or writing letters home. On the southern edge of the Bois de Sedan pioneers and infantry are repairing a bridge, clearing minefields and removing barbed wire barricades.*
>
> *13.00hr. Runners bring the order: Company commanders to HQ.*
>
> *This is at a crossroads. The commander sits surrounded by his officers. Orders from regiment have just been received: 'The 2nd Battalion will lead the advance across the Meuse, will break through the Maginot Line and go on to take Point 247.' The CO's voice is hard. Maps are marked up. 'The battalion will move out of its form-up area at 14.00hr. No. 7 Company will cross the Meuse here near this factory on the western side of Sedan and will be supported by the assault Pioneers. No. 6 Company will follow.'*
>
> *The companies move hurrying to cross the 10km of no-man's-land which separates us from the Meuse in the two hours which we have been given. All our equipment, ammunition and weapons have to be carried toiling up heights and down valleys. But these soldiers accomplish it, despite the glowing heat.*
>
> *At our feet lies the valley of the Meuse; there to the left Sedan is burning, directly in front of us Floing, and to the south our objective. Wherever we look nothing but explosions as fresh squadrons of Stukas bomb the enemy.*
>
> *We pass through Floing, checking left and right, but no shot sounds. Once on the main road we swing left and reach our factory. Now the French, realising the danger, have taken up the fight. The Pioneers with the assault boats cannot reach the river. Despite the good cover the enemy can see all our movements from his pill boxes. Help is needed. Assault guns roll forward but cannot break the reinforced concrete until heavy flak silences the enemy. Wounded are brought back. The flak enters the battle again and the first waves of the leading company cross the Meuse quickly just as we had practised it during the winter.*
>
> *Before us about 4km distant is Point 247 whose eastern side is our company objective. Hardly had the first platoons moved out from the river bank than fire was opened upon them. The groups made their way forward as if they were on a parade ground, threw hand grenades into the positions and stormed forward. The first French go to the rear with their hands raised. Onward: the efforts of the past days have been forgotten; the Grenadiers have an objective – Point 247. The first houses in the suburbs are fought through. On, on, keep going, we have not yet reached the pill boxes. There are shots. Are the French going to hold us here? Resistance is quickly broken. More and more prisoners go back.*
>
> *The railway line from Sedan to Mezieres is crossed and the Sedan/Donchery road is reached. A look to the left shows that the great road bridge has been blown. To the right we can see elements of No. 7 Company pinned down by fire. We must act. For No. 6 Company; there is only one solution to the problem. Attack!*
>
> *Reconnaissance shows there is a large bunker about 200m south of the road on the edge of an orchard and a smaller pill box about 250m half right behind the larger one.*
>
> *A brief battle and the bunker is reached. Hand grenades smoke the enemy out. The French*

stand with their backs to the wall and raise their hands: Tirez – shoot. They had been told that the Germans would shoot all Frenchmen caught in pill boxes.

The artillery fire becomes more severe. We are quite alone. There can be no pause; the objective must be taken in daylight. Then the road will be clear for the Panzers to reach into the rear areas of the Maginot Line. The enemy must be given no rest. The attack continues. The second pill box is taken and we can make out the anti-tank gun position. New assault troops are brought forward, the machine gun group fights down the riflemens' positions on the left and enables the company to move forward. We make contact with a rifle regiment moving forward on our right. This is a machine gun group which tells us that its regiment lies about 500m farther right of them and about level with us. The two heavy machine guns are a welcome support to the last part of the attack. Once again the Grenadiers move out. They climb the slope, through deeply cratered countryside, cross deep barbed wire barriers until the French open heavy defensive fire from behind a ridge. Machine gun and machine pistols send out their death-bringing bullets. Hand grenades explode; nobody pays any attention to the enemy fire. There is no time to stop. The leading troops are already in the enemy's position. Close combat fighting, hand to hand, with a wild swing the attack is driven forward.

Point 247 is ours; The way to the south has been opened!

The sombre words of *Oberleutnant* von Coubiere tell nothing of the feelings of those who undertake a river crossing under fire. One account was that of an assault Pioneer whose company had failed to make one assault crossing after which, of the fifty-two craft employed, only two remained operational. The account continues with a sergeant of Pioneers assembling No. 3 Group for the next assault.

Now the men have reached the stadium in Sedan. The enemy has woken from his paralysis and opens fire. How shall we get out of the building? There is a hole in the wall and through this No. 3 Group crawls to the river bank

From the bunkers on the far bank machine guns sweep the assault areas with their fire. The Meuse is 80 metres wide here.

The two assault craft are made ready, three-man boats which will have to carry four men. Will the three-man boat be able to carry such a burden? Throw away everything that is not absolutely necessary. Bangalore torpedoes are unnecessary. We don't need spades, we shan't have time to dig in, even if we get to the other side.

Embark! The boats are thrown into the water and the men fall into them. Water laps the gunwales. A little deeper in the water and the boat would sink.

The little boat starts to turn on its axis. They are not moving from the bank until the sergeant takes the rudder. Open fire; the loopholes in the pill box near to the river bank must be neutralised.

A bump – the bank is reached and the sergeant rushes towards a pill box and another Pioneer leaps on to its roof.

An explosive charge is slid through the loophole and blows up with a deafening roar; the men in the pill box open the heavy armoured door and pour out as a Pioneer throws in a hand grenade.

A Sturmgeschütz III, France 1940.

In this way the men of Infantry Regiment Grossdeutschland crossed and gained within hours a river line which the French had calculated would hold for a week at least. While 2nd Battalion had been fighting for Point 247, the other battalions had been battling against attacks by French tanks from 3rd Armoured Division, but those, although carried out with determination and bravery, were unco-ordinated and each was destroyed.

The German advance had smashed a gap between 2nd and 9th French Armies and Guderian's Panzer Corps, driving through the breach, had wheeled and placed itself on a line directed towards the English Channel. This move exposed Corps' left wing and to protect this Guderian moved the Grossdeutschland Regiment and 10th Panzer Division.

The military emphasis now moved so far as Grossdeutschland was concerned from the Meuse to Stonne, 20km due south of Sedan and set in rolling, wooded countryside. For a few brief days in May 1940 the little village had a great military value for whichever side held it could ensure the success of his operations. The French needed to retain it as a link between their two shattered armies while, to the Germans, it was the gateway to the next phase of the campaign: the armoured *blitzkrieg* drive to the sea

French armour and infantry attacks struck the Grossdeutschland Companies and the battle continued throughout the long afternoon. The number of casualties grew as both sides, aware of the importance of the village, flung their men into the bitter and desperate fighting.

It was not until dawn on 16 May that a regimental battle group stormed into Stonne and held it until late afternoon when 29th Division relieved it and Grossdeutschland went into reserve.

The subsequent weeks of the campaign are a chronicle of pursuit battles fought at first in West Flanders, around Dunkirk from which port the British Expeditionary Force was being evacuated and then, south of the Somme, driving southwards against crumbling French resistance until the Armistice was signed on 15 June.

The campaign in the west was over and in Europe there seemed to be no immediate enemy – always excepting the British. But they were weak and seemingly incapable of being or ever becoming a serious military threat. The German forces were, therefore, reduced in size as demobilisation of a number of regiments and divisions took place and some soldiers of that short, victorious campaign against the West returned to the civilian world. Peace might, it seemed, after all, be just around the corner in the new year of 1941.

Three
Infantry Regiment
Grossdeutschland's Second Campaign:
The Eastern Front, 1941-1942

'Army Group Timoshenko will be smashed before the onset of winter and Army Group Centre will carry out a double encirclement at Vyasma, using armoured forces on both flanks. After this encircling operation has been completed…a pursuit battle in the direction of Moscow.'
OKW Instruction No. 35, 6 September 1941

Following the fall of France the regiment was briefly involved in training for the invasion of the United Kingdom and then had a minor role in the 1941 Balkan campaign before it was moved eastwards towards the political struggle against the Soviet Union for which Hitler had begun to plan as early as the autumn of 1940.

During that campaign Grossdeutschland rose from an Infantry Regiment to a Panzer Corps and spent most of its active service life on the Eastern Front. From the mid-summer of 1941 to the early summer of 1945 the Infantry Regiment, then Division and finally Panzer Corps Grossdeutschland, and its constituent units served almost continuously against the Soviet Union. It is, therefore, important that the areas in which they battled as well as the army against which they fought be fully explained.

To express the war against the USSR in its simplest terms, Germany, with a population

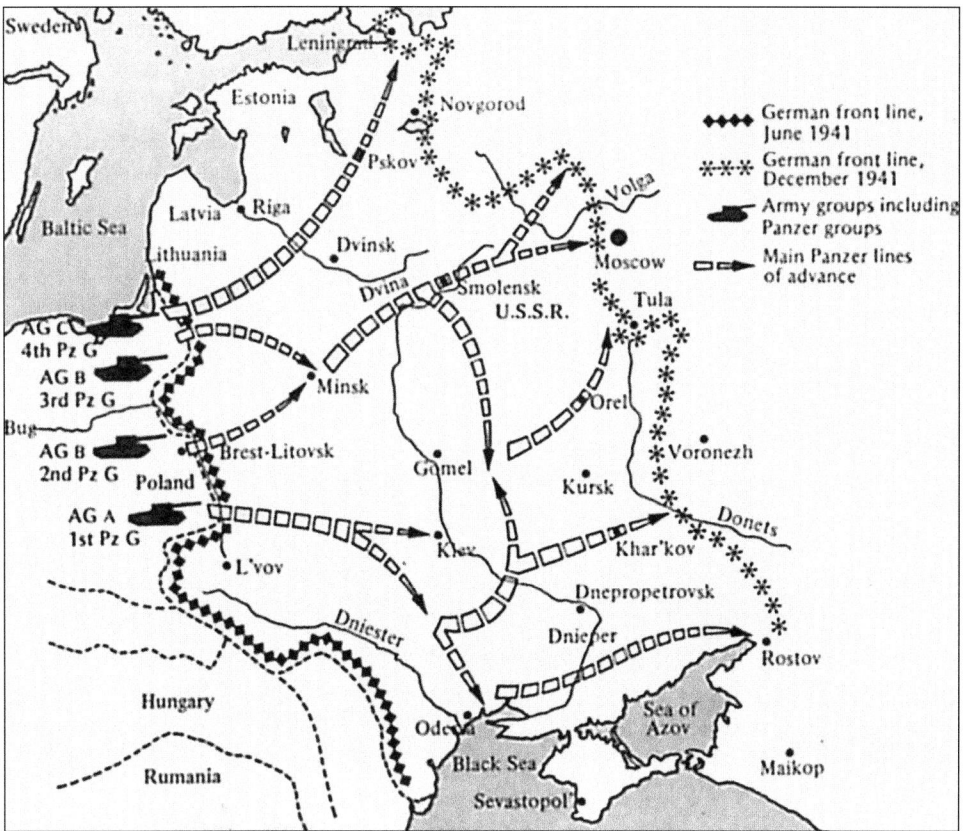

Operation Barbarossa.

of 80 million and, therefore, with limited manpower resources, was challenging the Soviet Union with a population of 170 million, inhabiting the greatest land mass on the globe. The Communist Party controlled the Soviet system and had in the Red Army a political/military weapon and a powerful instrument of party will. By the ruthless conscription of all available resources that Army, four million strong in peacetime, could be expanded in war to number ten million soldiers and kept at that peak, armed by an industry which could draw upon almost inexhaustible supplies of coal, iron, oil and wheat.

The campaign which the German Armed Forces began against the USSR on Sunday 22 June 1941, was without doubt one of the greatest military operations in the history of warfare and, at the same time, one of the most ill-conceived. The compulsion to destroy the Soviet state blinded Hitler to every other consideration and he refused either to recognise or to countenance any suggestion, however militarily valid, which in his opinion obstructed or delayed this political aim.

Planning for the war against the USSR had begun almost immediately after the campaign against France and one draft drawn up by *Major-General* Marcks, Chief of Staff to 18th Army, was rejected by Hitler. A new plan drawn up by *Major-General* Friedrich von

Paulus, Chief of Staff to the Army's High Command, was accepted and his proposals formed the basis for Plan *Barbarossa*.

As the Third Reich was neither militarily nor economically capable of fighting an intense, protracted war the purpose of the approaching campaign would have to be for a 'quick knock-out'. This might have been achieved by a concentration of maximum strength at critical points to attain absolutely vital objectives. But what were they? Hitler, the Supreme Commander, would give no clear directives and allowed vague economic premises to influence his military judgements; indeed, he was not above allowing sudden intuitions to alter his battle plan. In the early days of the fighting he was to interfere with the progress of a battle seeking to obtain easy, tactical victories instead of pursuing a firm and logical strategy. Later he was to take over the whole direction of military operations both strategic and tactical; but this is to anticipate events. From the outset there had been little clear idea of the final objectives of the war apart from a long-term aim of manning a defensive barrier from the Volga to Arkangelsk, against the USSR. This was to follow upon the defeat of the Red Army. But how the Soviet forces were to be defeated was the cause of basic and fundamental differences of opinion in both *Oberkommando* des Heeres (OKH – Army High Command) and OKW. The deepest division was in the OKH's opposition to Hitler's plan to achieve a strategic victory on both flanks: in the north against Leningrad and to the south in the Ukraine. It was the firm conviction of the professional commanders that a decision must be sought and obtained in the centre – i.e., Moscow must be the principal objective. This concept Hitler totally rejected.

There are four considerations which must be taken into account in the planning and execution of a battle. These are; the strength of one's own forces, those of the enemy, the terrain and the climate. Conscious of their own army's strength the German Command underestimated the second factor, was ill-informed about the third and disregarded the fourth.

The Infantry Regiment Grossdeutschland with whom we are concerned served for much of its life with Army Group Centre and thus it is the terrain of the region in which the regiment fought which will be described here. The future battlefield was White Russia. This was an area with a poor communications network and with few hard-surfaced, all-weather roads so that the railways, although few in number, assumed a strategic importance not present in the other campaigns. Possession of these tracks was vital for supply and reinforcement, even though the gauge of the rails was different to that in use in Western Europe and the procurement, maintenance and modification of rolling stock was to become and to remain a major task for the officers of the Army's supply and engineering corps.

There were two natural avenues of advance. The northern one led from Warsaw through Minsk and Smolensk to Moscow; the southern one extended from Lemberg to the Ukraine and the Caucasus. Covering the territory between these two land bridges was a vast and impassable natural obstacle, the Pripet Marshes and crossing the territory on a general north-west to south-easterly line were four major rivers which also formed barriers to an east-west advance. These four waterways were the Dnieper, with its tributaries the Drut, Beresina, Sosch and Pripet; the Duna with the Obal, Drissa and Lutkosa forming its tributaries; the Lovats, running on an almost north-south line and, lastly the Niemen.

Much of the terrain between the rivers was covered by vast and extensive forests of such density that they could be considered as primeval. These jungles covered more than twenty-five per cent of the total land area and restricted panzer movement, channelling the advance into predictable areas which could be easily defended.

The military planners of the OKH, basing their strategy upon past campaigns fought over the extensive communications network of western Europe and, in anticipation of a short war, omitted from their calculations the effect that climatic conditions might have upon the new enterprise. As a generalisation it would be true to say that even under the most favourable terrain conditions the climate exerted a tremendous influence upon operations. Two hours' rain was sufficient to turn a so-called highway into a mud track. The dust of summer scoured the engines of German vehicles which, unlike the Soviet versions, were not fitted with a fine dust filter. Lacking this elementary piece of equipment German engines had only a short life and a poor performance; the engineering workshops were always full of vehicles under repair and most units had only half or even less of their vehicle establishment as 'runners' at any given time.

The Soviet winter was long and hard producing temperatures so far below zero that motor engines and weapons frequently froze solid, and the east wind whipped up blizzards whose intensity restricted movement to a minimum. However during the winter there were days or even weeks of thaw during which time the snow melted and turned the ground into a morass. A similar condition was produced during the spring thaw and vehicles trapped in the tenacious mud could often not be towed out by tractors or tanks and had to be left until frost or the sun had hardened the ground. The duration of real campaigning weather was thus very short.

Let us consider now another underestimated factor – the Red Army. Compared with the Wehrmacht which had behind it four short, successful campaigns, the Soviet force had only the humiliations of the war with Finland. German military morale was high as a result of its victories; the Red Army and particularly the High Command was recovering from the mass murders which had been carried out against the Officer Corps during the great Stalin purges of 1936-7.

German Intelligence appreciations believed that serious defects in the senior echelons of command in the Soviet Army were directly attributable to those years of blood-letting and listed these faults as slowness, lack of decision and inadequate organisation. The same Memorandum did, however, pay tribute to the fighting ability of the ordinary soldier, his endurance, tenacity and offensive spirit even in the most hopeless situations.

One disadvantage of Red Army training was that its commanders had had no instruction in withdrawal or disengagement operations – all their plans were based upon advance and attack – and lacking such preparation their forces were held, surrounded and destroyed by faster moving German forces.

Grüppenführer Max Simon, in his paper on *Soviet Russian Infantry and Armoured Forces,* when discussing the Red Infantry says of them:

> …*the officers…exercise firm authority over their regiments and are able to create from the mass under them a manoeuvrable body, the individual members of which will hug the terrain when*

working their way forward, will quickly dig in and as quickly push forward again or allow themselves to be slaughtered if so ordered. The native frugality of the Russian and Asiatic not only favours the restriction of the supply train of combat troops to a minimum, but also makes it possible to exploit the strength of the individual in a measure which seems impossible to the European. The insensitivity of the men to weather conditions, their craftiness and closeness to nature, likewise facilitate training and increases the value of the infantry.

The simple needs of the Communist soldier are also reflected in his equipment. A lightweight suit in summer, a padded jacket and trousers in the winter…sturdy leather waterproof boots for the summer and simple winter boots which are made of felt…Cooking utensils, a wooden spoon and shaving equipment are all that is taken along besides weapons and ammunition.

The advantages and disadvantages inherent in the national characteristics peculiar to the peoples of the Soviet Union naturally set their imprint on the tactics employed. On the one hand will be found a clever utilisation of terrain…ruthlessness and mercilessness towards friend and foe. On the other hand will be found a rigid adherence to decisions once made and a stubborn insistence on carrying out plans…

The German attack upon the Soviet Union should have come as no surprise to the Soviet leaders. The British Government had sent them accurate warnings and a Communist cell within the German forces had telegraphed the date and the hour of the attack. Nevertheless no preparation seems to have been made to warn the troops lining the frontier of the ensuing war and, indeed, until the last minutes before the first barrage opened, a Soviet train entered the German zone of Poland, loaded with grain; part of the trade agreement between the two countries.

Although, in the short term, the Red Army had been surprised, in the long term the Soviet government had made adequate preparations and from the outbreak of the Second World War, the Soviets had undertaken an arms drive of enormous proportions. The production of all types of weapons increased but nowhere was this advance so pronounced as in the manufacture of armoured fighting vehicles.

Guderian, Germany's panzer expert, had estimated as early as 1937 that the Red Army had a force of 10,000 tanks and had forecast even before the opening of the war against the Soviet Union, that she would have 17,000 vehicles on establishment. Post-war research by American military authorities has shown that even that figure was too low and that there were actually 23,000 machines on the Red Army strength. Such achievements in production gave the Red Army a superiority in armour of at least three to one while in artillery and particularly in infantry the imbalance was even greater.

Tremendous strides were made to re-equip the infantry with new firearms but despite this the majority at the outbreak of the German-Soviet War was still equipped with the 1930 variant of the 1891 rifle. A new carbine was introduced in 1938, but reliance was still laid, according to the *History of the Great Soviet Fatherland War,* 'upon the Degtjaryov light machine-gun and the obsolescent Maxim heavy machine-gun'. The Degtjaryov machine-pistol came in during 1940 and semi-automatic, self-loading rifles at about the same time but these were not being produced in sufficient numbers to equip even the front line troops. The Shpagin pistol, probably the world's finest weapon of the period, came in during the first half of 1941 and, due to the simplicity of its design and its robust construction was very soon in mass production.

Even before the Second World War began consideration given to the production of artillery and armour had produced guns with high muzzle velocity. Among these were the 7.6cm 1939 Field Gun, the 12.2cm 1938 Howitzer and the 15.2cm gun/howitzer 1937 pattern. Soviet anti-tank guns which went into production in late 1938 had a power of penetration that enabled them to 'kill' any armoured fighting vehicle put against them. The Soviet tank arm had made great strides during the period from 1936 to 1939 and the products of that enterprise soon made their appearance upon the battlefield.

The KV (Klimenti Voroshilov) and more especially the T34, the standard armoured fighting vehicles of the Red Army, gave to the Soviets a qualitative superiority for they were better, in almost every respect, than the German panzerwagen and were proof against the best German anti-tank gun of the period. The only advantages which the Germans could bring against these tanks when they first met them were their greater skill – having handled their vehicles in other campaigns – superior tactics and rapid communications between individual vehicles and the command tank. Soviet communications' systems – where such existed – were unreliable and the tactical handling of the armoured units in the early days was poor. The destruction of a command vehicle effectively destroyed Soviet resistance whereas a similar occurrence within a German panzer unit caused only temporary difficulty.

The organisation of the Red Army in the spring of 1941 was an arrangement of Military or Special Military Districts along the western, i.e. German/Soviet, frontier. Shortly after the outbreak of war these military districts were re-formed and renamed as fronts: the North-eastern, the North-western, Western, South-western and Southern Fronts. Three of the old Bolshevik commanders during the Revolution were given supreme command: Marshal Klimenti Voroshilov, Marshal Semen K. Timoshenko and Marshal Semen M. Budenny and the defeats of the first months of the war are associated with these men.

Facing the military colossus of the Soviet Union was a German Army from whose grand total of 194 divisions (1941 figure) no fewer than 59 would have to be drawn off to garrison occupied Europe and to fight in North Africa. This would make a weak battle line, even at the opening of the campaign, but then as the Army Groups making the assault advanced into the USSR proper the front would begin to increase in length. The law of diminishing returns would then come into play for with a longer line to man, coupled with the losses which could be expected from the fighting there would be, inevitably, fewer and fewer soldiers to hold back an enemy whose numbers would increase as his mobilisation reached its peak.

Military logic must have been against this desperate gamble unless overwhelming proof existed that the Soviet masses were ripe for a revolution which could be precipitated by the destruction of the Red Army. Hitler had no doubts as to the conditions in the USSR and was firm in his conviction that 'one has only to smash the door in and the whole rotten edifice will collapse'.

But the Soviet Union was an enigma and neither the OKW nor the Army's General Staff had accurate or detailed information on her political, social, military or economic conditions. Lacking such positive intelligence with which to contradict Hitler's optimism and, in the face of the Führer's buoyant confidence, the High Command military appreciations took the line of least resistance and followed Hitler's lead. The new enemy's strength and fighting capacity were, therefore, both wildly underestimated.

Three German Army Groups formed for the new war were North (von Leeb), Centre (von Bock) and South (von Rundstedt). The total of these forces, together with the OKH reserve, amounted to 106 infantry divisions, 19 panzer and 10 motorised divisions. To augment this mass of power, Germany's allies volunteered contingents from their national armies and these numbered just over fourteen divisions of infantry and/or cavalry.

The army groups had Leningrad, Moscow and the Ukraine as their respective objectives and these were to be seized before going on to capture and to hold the eastern line. Thus the first bounds which the Armies had to make were enormous ones. The objective of Army Group South, for example, was nearly 700 miles from the frontier and that of Army Group Centre was nearly as far.

In this, the account of the first campaign which Grossdeutschland was to fight in the USSR, we are concerned only with Army Group Centre. Its establishment was: 2nd and 3rd Panzer Groups, 4th and 9th Army. We are to follow Guderian's Panzer Group 2, attached to 4th Army, and which had four Corps on establishment: the 12th, the 24th and the 46th in which the Infantry Regiment Grossdeutschland served. The last corps on Guderian's establishment, was the 47th.

During the spring of 1941, the German divisions and corps moved into position along and behind the river Bug which marked the frontier between the territories of the Third Reich and of the Soviet Union. By mid-May the build-up was in full swing with an average of three hundred trains per day bringing forward the vast amounts of material which would be needed to nourish the armies and to sustain the advance. By June all the assaulting troops were in position. More than half a million motor vehicles had been grouped and three quarters of a million horses, as well as over seven thousand pieces of artillery had been brought together for a war which, according to Josef Goebbels was to cause 'the whole world to hold its breath'.

Plans had been drawn up, the armies were in position, the stores had been assembled and with high hopes in their hearts the soldiers of the German Army waited for the dawn of Sunday, 22 June 1941 to break for, with the sunrise of that historic day, would open another campaign which they expected would finish as quickly and as gloriously as had the others in which they had fought.

The war on the Eastern Front falls into four main phases. The first of these extends from the invasion of the USSR and covers the Soviet winter counter-offensive. The second phase sees the German summer offensive of 1942, which was to strike southwards at the Caucasus and eastwards to seize Stalingrad; but at that city on the Volga the great assault was held and flung back. After the failure of the 1943 summer offensive whose principal aim was to pinch out the salient at Kursk, the Germans lost the military initiative, the Soviets gained the upper hand and opened a series of operations which were to push the Wehrmacht westwards. The final phase begins with the withdrawal of the German Army from the areas in the Balkans and Central Europe which it had occupied and ends with the final struggles fought as the British and American advances entered Germany from the west and the great battle for Berlin during April and May 1945. The war against the Soviet Union had been lost and the depth of the defeat of the German Army was the parade and public humiliation in Red Square of those of its regimental colours which had been captured in Berlin.

Grossdeutschland enters the campaign

The barrage which opened at 03.15hr along the 1,500-mile-long front did not call the men of the Infantry Regiment Grossdeutschland immediately to battle and it was not until a week of the campaign had passed before the unit crossed the Bug river.

The regiment's first task was to thicken the infantry line around the Soviet troops trapped in a vast pocket. Long marches, constant patrolling and fierce battles to fling back the Red Army occupied the days and nights of the Grenadiers.

Soviet probes to find weak spots in the German pincers were constant and the regiment was frequently called upon to force-march to where some hard-pressed battalion was holding back a Soviet flood and by determined, aggressive action to force back within the ring of encirclement the Soviet troops who would flee it. Soviet counter-attacks using both infantry and armour frequently forced the Grenadiers on to the defensive and only immediate counter-attacks could repel the incursions and restore the line.

The fighting in which Grossdeutschland was involved was not the severe and desperate struggles like those in the trenches of the First World War, but was nerve racking in the uncertainty of the enemy's location and exhausting in the ferocity of the short but fierce battles brought against a fanatical and implacable foe. Its duties in the line were of police/security type interspersed with savage fighting. Patrols roamed through the thick undergrowth, each man fully aware of the skill in fieldcraft and sniping of their Red Army opponents. Nerves were stretched taut as the groups moved slowly, and very cautiously through dense and matted vegetation. Here and there there would be a sudden burst of shots, disturbing the heavy heat of the long July days as a sniper was dealt with. Suddenly, out of the bushes, only a short distance ahead of the patrol group a line of khaki uniformed Red Army men would spring up. In the first shock the question would strike each Grenadier: will these Bosheviks give up or attack? Almost invariably and immediately the coarse, long drawn and throaty 'Hooray' of the Soviet battle cry would roar out and soon the Red Army men would be at close quarters. Then it was the frantic struggle with knife and bayonet; the stabbing and the hacking until as sudden as had been their appearance so as quick was the disappearance of the Soviet soldiers. Or else a walk along a path used ten times before and a sudden shot as another sniper who had infiltrated the area claimed a victim requiring a patrol of tired soldiers to be sent to flush him out.

By night the Soviet feint assaults to draw fire; infiltration into the Grenadier positions; sudden showers of hand grenades; Rata the little night bomber with its load of lethal anti-personnel bombs; and the losses, always the losses, suffered but never replaced in full, so that sentry duties came round more often to men exhausted from patrolling and from withstanding counter-attacks.

Dimly across the vast fields and thick forests came the hum of lorries as along the roads heading eastwards the bulk of von Kluge's Army and Guderian's Panzer Group roared towards newer, vaster encirclements, their line of advance guarded from attack by the

Grenadiers carrying out their vital but unglamorous tasks.

At last came the chance to escape from the monotonously dangerous task of policing the road forward and the regiment was called up to add weight to the battles to break the Dnieper line and to undertake a river crossing like that across the Meuse more than a year before. The attack went in at dawn on 11 July, and the river was crossed.

The subsequent fighting on the far bank was bitter and the battle line swayed backwards and forwards as villages were torn from the Grenadiers' grasp and then recaptured again in breathless counter-attacks launched in a stifling heat. The insistent Soviet snipers infiltrated the front and worked their way into the vast fields of sunflowers which covered that area of White Russia. Lethal games of hide and seek, with death or mutilation as the penalty for failure, were played out in the long green tunnels below the nodding golden flower heads.

Throughout the long, hot days the Soviet troops were put straight into battle as they arrived in the Grossdeutschland regimental sector, and their strength increased with each passing hour. As the Soviet power grew so did that of the German force diminish. The companies were losing men and only by amalgamation of rifle groups and platoons could a defence be maintained. As the German line grew thinner the distance between positions widened and on one occasion through those gaps Red Army patrols were able to penetrate and make wider breaches into which new attacks poured, overwhelming infantry slit trenches and often threatening the artillery positions. To hold back the Red tide from the gun line Grenadiers from regimental rear echelon units dug in around the artillery pieces. Across the open and slightly undulating ground the Red troops advanced and were struck by a barrage fired by gunners who knew that their lives depended upon the speed with which they could load and fire. The Soviet first lines recoiled and even as they hesitated new flights of shells struck them until at first slowly but then with an ever increasing tempo the attack flooded back.

By 15 July the Soviet force was unable to obtain more men, having failed in one last furious attack deserters began to come in, Red Army men who had resisted with a determination which bordered on fanaticism suddenly broke and began to surrender in such numbers that more than 17,000 were taken.

All through the days and weeks of early autumn the German advance was pushed forward against the most determined resistance and continual Soviet counter-attacks which came in with incredible rigidity, reminiscent of the offensives of the First World War; waves of men advancing, rolling forward making no attempt to deploy and not varying the timetable of their assaults. As one attack was smashed into the ground the survivors were regrouped and put back into the assault. The Soviet infantry were poured into the battle, the living advancing across ground covered with the fallen of previous failed assaults and the whole time massive bombardments by the artillery trying hard to smash the German ring which encircled them on three sides.

The need to keep the German front line units supplied with the essential needs of war meant that there were many days on which no food or water came up to the forward positions and on several occasions even the supply of artillery shells failed. Then for much of the time the Grenadiers were forced to endure barrages from Soviet guns to which their own artillery could make at best an ineffectual and, at other times, no reply at all.

Red Army infantry taken prisoner during the 1942 summer offensive.

The situation which the regiment had suffered along the Dnieper was repeating itself: the companies were bleeding to death as casualties were not replaced. Day in, day out the Soviet attacks continued. Night brought no respite and the signal rockets rose from the German front lines, their red flare announcing some fresh attack by enemy infantry or, more urgent still, the violet signal light which told that the Grenadier line was under assault by Red armour.

Those who fought in the first battles of the new campaign against the Soviet Union recall each fight as one of a series of bloody milestones; the Dnieper, the Yelnya river and then the cutting off of the Red armies in the giant encirclement at Kiev. In each of these, but particularly the last, there was such a heavy blood toll that time and again the regiment was all but destroyed.

During the marching and fighting connected with the Kiev salient battles Grossdeutschland had, served both as a sword and as a shield cutting its way through Red Army units and defences or defending against persistent counter-attack the open flank of Guderian's panzer group. Even when the encirclement had been completed the fighting continued at a more furious tempo as the trapped Soviet units struggled to break out.

By the beginning of October with two great encirclement battles already in progress at Briansk and at Vyasma the German High Command then set new objectives for Army

Group Centre and Guderian's 2nd Panzer Army was ordered to capture Tula, the last major obstacle before Moscow.

For its part in an investment operation east of Briansk the Infantry Regiment Grossdeutschland was ordered on 11 October to contain Soviet attempts to escape from encirclement through the vast jungle-like forests of that area.

The widely spread out companies and strong points of the Infantry Regiment Grossdeutschland, were now involved in jungle warfare where visibility was measured in feet. The crisis point was reached during the end of the second week of October when the whole regiment was heavily engaged in fighting back the Red masses and in pushing northwards to compress the Soviets into a tighter pocket.

There was much snow now and across the clearings in the jungle the Grenadiers struck but were held off from one Soviet position at Karachev. The Grenadiers dug in to await the reinforcement and support which would be needed if the advance was to continue. Even when this came up the fighting was still bitter and long. Soviet snipers and mortar fire, the Katyusha barrages with their steel fragments slicing through the air and cutting down whole batches of men charging forward into the attack made each step of the advance a martyrdom. Before the Red line had been reached nearly every officer and senior NCO of the assault companies had been killed or wounded and the attack was pressed home by junior corporals and private soldiers. With astonishing persistence the Grossdeutschland Grenadiers thrust and thrust and thrust again until at last the Soviet resistance cracked and the battle was nearly over.

On the desolate and snow covered battlefield there were hundreds of guns, carts, soft skin and armoured vehicles burning, destroyed or abandoned among the trees. Columns of prisoners, their morale broken, marched into captivity. Their captors, the Grenadiers of Infantry Regiment Grossdeutschland stood watching them pass without emotion. The battle of Karachev, fought on 14 and 15 October 1941, had drained them completely and left them exhausted, cold and hungry in the sudden silence of the vast dark forests.

The fine weather of September had long since given way to days of rain which foretold the onset of winter and the roads became streams of mud impassable to anything but infantry and armour. The great sodden steppes and wide expanses of the central Soviet Union stretched, seemingly unending, before the German troops and only the knowledge that at last the Army was heading for Moscow animated the tired and overstretched soldiers. The great double encirclement battles of Briansk and Vyasma had been completed by 19 October. Only Tula now remained and behind Tula lay Moscow.

Infantry Regiment Grossdeutschland was brought forward on 24 October to co-operate with 3rd Panzer Division in an attempt to revive an attack by 2nd Panzer Division which had been held by fanatical Soviet resistance. Deeply conscious of the importance of Tula to the defence of the Soviet capital the Red Army troops fought with skill and determination and flung back the Grenadier attack to its start line within an hour of opening the assault. Regrouped and covered by Stukas the regiment moved forward again to storm the heights to the north-west of the town.

The fighting was fierce but successful and with the objective seemingly secure in German hands the Grenadier battalions pushed forward towards a new objective, the town of Cherno.

On Sunday, 26 October 1941, while the Grossdeutschlaad Regiment was fighting in and around Cherno, 2nd Panzer Army had reached the Oka river smashing three Soviet divisions which had opposed it. Although later in that month the Corps struck and defeated three other Red divisions in its thrust towards Tula, the advance was slowing down. One of the Soviet Union's oldest allies, 'General Mud', had made his presence felt and in the Panzer Army sector more than 2,000 vehicles were held fast and immobile in the gripping slime. Only the infantry could move but even their advances were physical battles against the weight of the mud which clung to boots and trousers, and was often so tenacious that it sucked off the jackboots from the feet. Very slowly the German advance crept towards Tula.

It was with 3rd Panzer Division that Grossdeutschland was selected to make the assault which would take out the town. On 29 October the attack began to roll. Past the great woods outside Tula driving along roads cratered with mine explosions; nothing was allowed to halt the pace of the advance as the armoured columns converged on to the town. The Panzers rumbled across a small bridge, into a sunken lane and were trapped. The armour unable to withdraw had to fight its way through detachments of Red Army soldiers and men of the local militia who fought the vehicles with Molotov cocktails and with explosive charges. Thus it was not until nightfall that the outskirts of Tula were reached. The weary tank crews and their Grenadier escorts taking up all-round positions to protect them throughout the night could note with satisfaction that their 45km advance had brought them through an area held in great strength and defended with great heroism by Soviet soldiers and citizens.

'Stand to', at dawn on 30th was followed by a hasty breakfast, for the field kitchens had not yet kept pace with the swift advance. Then the battalions moved off again through the wooden shacks of the villages and suburbs of Tula towards the great blocks of buildings which marked the newer, inner city. Armour is not the best weapon to fight in built-up areas and the pace of the advance towards the city centre began to slow and finally was brought to a halt in front of a vast block of flats.

There was now little coherence or power in the German assault. Machine gun groups had had to be dropped off to hold street crossings or to assault some particularly well-defended house and these continual drains reduced combat strength to a point at which there were only sixty men in the forward unit; too few to maintain the offensive. There could be no fresh advance; it was now their only task to defend and hold the positions. Shortly before nightfall small groups of Grenadiers gathered in shell holes, in ruined buildings or behind walls and took up positions for all-round defence. The wireless sets had long since ceased to be of any use in this built-up area; the Soviet telephone lines were down and the Army sets with their frail and vulnerable wires could not maintain a permanent or continuous link. The groups of Grenadiers isolated from each other could communicate only by using runners who traversed the dangerous and bullet-swept streets, or by signal flares fired at intervals to indicate the forward positions.

During the morning of 31 October multi-barrelled mortars poured a barrage up on the German positions and behind this fierce rain of fire Red infantry advanced to the assault armed with bayonets and grenades. In their first thrust they over-rolled outpost positions but at other points along the roughly formed perimeter there was hand to hand fighting until the Grenadiers forced back the Red infantry and smashed them.

With the failure of their infantry attacks, the Reds then sent in armour but the Grenadiers could now use in the confined areas those tactics which the Soviets had used against the German panzer. Tank hunting teams went out to search for and to destroy the Soviet vehicles. Throughout the succeeding nights Red assaults came in; at times with, and at other times without, tank support. The incessant bombardments, the repeated attacks, casualties and the strain of fighting reduced the battalions but no relief from the line could be afforded them at that time. Nor could the projected attack upon Tula go in. The armoured fighting vehicles had outrun their fuel supplies and the machines were immobile pill boxes; targets of every long range Soviet artillery piece.

There was only one logical solution, bitter though it was. On 9 November the remnants of the Grossdeutschland battalions and the survivors of 3rd Panzer Division evacuated the Tula region. The resistance of Boldin's 50th Red Army had been too great for them to overcome; the town had been converted into a fortress, the Soviet 4th Tank Brigade had been flung into battle and the intervention of that unit, against the unmanoeuvrable German armour and the depleted infantry, had turned the scales. Retreat was the only course of action and the road back from Tula was marked by columns of black smoke where panzer crews destroyed their fuelless vehicles rather than have them fall into the hands of the Soviets.

By this time it was no longer a battle against the Red Army; it was a struggle for survival. By the first week of November the ground was covered with a permanent frost and severe snow storms had begun. By night the temperatures dropped and to be caught on the open steppe was to die of exposure. Battles were fought for hamlets too small and too insignificant to be marked on road maps. There were even struggles for individual huts, for anything that would afford shelter from the biting icy wind and the razor sharp ice particles which covered everything living or dead with a sheet of ice.

The fighting was now restricted to the few short hours of daylight and to night patrols which went out to ensure that the immediate billeting area was not being infiltrated by Soviet troops. The German Army had no special clothing against the bitterness of the Soviet winter. Cap comforters and belly bands were the only protection for the soldiers in temperatures which had sunk a long way past zero. Complacency in the highest echelons of command in believing that no winter clothing would be required, coupled with an incompetence of the supply officers meant that thousands died of exposure and hundreds of thousands suffered limb amputations as a result of frostbite. One infantry battalion from 24th Corps had eight hundred cases of frostbite in a single day; eight times more than the numbers of killed, wounded and missing.

The lack of understanding on the part of the Supreme Command of true conditions at the front was beyond belief. Halder, at one point during the winter fighting, was to order 2nd Panzer Army which had been reduced to only 50 tanks from its establishment of 600, to drive forward and to reach the town of Gorky, an objective some 40km past Moscow.

Army Group Centre was starving. It required thirty-two trains per day if it were to receive its full quota, but it was a rare day indeed when more than twenty trainloads arrived at the vast depots in Smolensk. Thus there was a permanent shortage of food, fuel

The Red Army in attack.

and ammunition. Warm clothing was given such a low priority that only a minimum was brought forward and thus front line troops often had only one winter-lined coat between every five men. The difficulties of bringing clothing up to the infantry meant that the stocks which did arrive were issued first to rear echelon detachments while the rifle companies, sheltering in huts in isolated villages or even exposed for hours together on the open steppe and lacking even hot food, did not receive their protective clothing until the winter had nearly past.

The full story of the frightfulness of that first winter in the USSR has never been told, nor can it be imagined by anyone who has not themselves experienced life as an infantryman holding the trenches of a battle line during that season. Winter began prematurely in the late autumn of 1941 and was the coldest for one hundred years. Even the Soviet troops, properly clad and accustomed to the harsh climate, suffered terribly and were affected by the intense cold. One retreating German detachment which had sheltered overnight in a collection of huts passed without hindrance through a Soviet encirclement because the soldiers of the Red Army had spent the night on the open steppe and were so bemused by the cold that they had not the energy to intercept the Germans.

In such low temperatures slight wounds mortified and turned gangrenous as German bodies weak from the insufficient rations and the inhuman demands being made upon them lacked the strength to resist. With no facilities to wash, with no change of clothing, the whole army was vermin ridden, adding to the appalling conditions under which the front line soldier lived. In many units socks, continually wet from the snow and mud, had disintegrated completely, affording the bare feet no protection against frostbite. The climatic conditions were undoubtedly bad – the shortage of food was bearable, even the lack of adequate clothing could be tolerated but, overriding all these things there was always and everywhere the Red Army. The enemy which had been contesting with the Grossdeutschland Grenadiers were Siberian riflemen, picked soldiers, splendidly equipped, warmly clad and thoroughly at home in the Arctic conditions. Patrols of their ski troops swept through the defensive zones and attacked the billets in rear areas. Siberian snipers with unbelievable patience would wait for hours to obtain a clear shot; all the time wearing down the nerves of the German troops. This was truly a winter of discontent for the German Army.

Towards the end of November a new attack upon Tula was ordered. The German strategists, aware that any assault from the south or west would run up against the extensive defences which the Soviets had constructed, ordered 24th Corps to fight past and outflank the town and then to swing back and to attack it from the east to meet another thrust which would be made from the west. Between the two pincers Tula would be taken and Moscow might yet be reached before the depths of winter. The Infantry Regiment Grossdeutschland, taking part in this operation formed part of 3rd Panzer Division and opened the offensive on 3 December. Despite the best efforts of the Grenadiers the advance could not be brought forward, the assault petered out and although at one time the distance separating the two points of the encircling jaws was only 15km even this short distance was beyond the capacity of 24th Corps to attain. The night temperatures had now dropped to 37 degrees below zero, a cold so intense that tank engines could not be started and gun breeches froze solid and could not be opened.

On 5 December the Soviet counter-attack was launched by five Red Armies against a German force which stood exhausted along a winter line set out on the open steppeland. The Soviet intent was the isolation and destruction of Army Group Centre. The 2nd Panzer Army, anticipating the order from Army Group prepared to withdraw. By 7 December OKH realised that a withdrawal must be made if the Corps and Divisions of Army Group Centre were to be saved and confirmed the order.

Together with the remainder of the Army Group the Infantry Regiment Grossdeutschland began to give up that ground for which it had suffered and bled during the months of late autumn. But to disengage from a tenacious enemy who has no intention of allowing a chance to form a fresh defensive line is no easy task. Across the wide and open country Soviet cavalry and armour clung to the German rearguards, harrying and cutting off isolated units. Individual houses were turned into defensive positions from which the closely pursuing Soviets could be held off, the men of the small garrisons accepting full well the fact that they were doomed, but that their sacrifice would buy time for the regiment to escape. At night the fight for houses was even more essential for within their warmth sleep would come and an escape made from some of the horrors of the retreat. Those who captured the houses and huts survived; those who failed perished in the blizzards and the cold which now reached 45 degrees below zero.

By day the Grenadiers waded through snow drifts and across fields on which the snow lay thigh-deep and the physical strain soon exhausted them. Burdened down by their weapons, usually without food and fighting all the time, the Grenadiers marched westwards; and it was a question of march or die for death came to those who fell out too exhausted to continue the withdrawal.

Throughout those days of suffering the German Army moved back with little central control and Grenadier battalions were often seconded to other units to act as stiffeners in a battle line which was now brittle to breaking point. It was, however, not a story of continuous defeat for the SP Company, during one day's sharp burst of activity, destroyed fifteen Soviet tanks and the Anti-tank Company claimed its hundredth victim. But these minor victories could not hide the fact that it was a hard and bitter retreat.

On 16 December the Regiment came under severe Red pressure east of the main highway, near Kossaya. Across the wide open plain the Red troops swept forward, their camouflage jackets making them almost invisible against the snow, and supported by rocket bombardment flung themselves against the thin line of Grenadiers lying in holes hastily scraped from the snow. Where there had been time entrenching tools had cut chunks of ice and these had been erected to form both a wall and a parapet on which to rest the rifles and machine-guns. Firing was limited to bursts of short duration for the fingers of the riflemen were soon frozen by exposure to the open air. Again and again the Soviet troops came forward and as every attack receded the Grenadiers counted their own casualties and sent back for treatment those whom it would still help. Others, too badly wounded to endure the journey back to the first aid posts, stayed with the front line troops until they succumbed to their wounds. Slightly wounded men refused to leave, realising that every man withdrawn from the front placed a heavier burden upon those who remained. Then the Soviet troops stormed forward again, across the space now sullied with explosions and littered with dead, repeating the same tactics and adopting the same formations for every assault until the fire from the MG 34s drove them back and the mortars smashed their concentrations. At last even they were exhausted; it was all over and when it had finished 1st Battalion of the Infantry Regiment Grossdeutschland had been reduced to the strength of a single company.

All offensives eventually run out of steam and falter and the Soviet winter offensive of 1941 was no exception. On 21 December and for a short space of time the Soviet pressure relaxed and the Grenadier companies could sort themselves out and begin to reorganise. By this time the German High Command had recovered from its paralysis and had formed a defensive line along the river Oka. Soviet attacks then began to come in again, initiating battles fought in bitterly low temperatures. The temporary lull had been used by the Soviets to bring up more and more men to force a breakthrough of the German front. It was not unusual for the Soviet superiority to be so great that whole divisions were put in against a single Grossdeutschland battalion.

By the end of the first week of February preparations had begun to allow the German Army to go over to the counter-offensive. Over-extended as they were, the Red spearheads could offer no determined resistance to the German drive and they were flung back in disorder, moving further and further back and at an increasing pace until they had been driven from the main highway from Bolkov to Yagodnaya. The Soviet forward troops as well as those in the rear areas were in disarray and the tempo of the Grenadier advance increased in proportion to the chaos and disorder that they found. The Grossdeutschland Regiment, ever in the vanguard of the forward movement, was now able to inflict upon the Red rearguard the same harrying and thrusting manoeuvres to which they had been subjected only weeks before.

Then the German forces found that they were meeting more determined resistance and it was clear that Stavka, having overcome its surprise at the speed of the German reaction, had prepared its defences.

On 18 February the Grenadier battalions suffered such severe losses during their assaults upon Tsklovo that the strength of one battalion was reduced to sixty men, i.e. the establishment of a platoon. The regimental front line strength was eventually reduced to three officers and thirty other ranks. The Grossdeutschland Infantry Regiment was almost dead.

The abortive attack against Tsklovo was the last attempt which the regiment made during that winter. The arrival of reinforcements and the return of convalescents did bring the regiment back to a respectable size but it was a unit without any armour for during one Soviet assault on 29 February the last remaining SP gun on regimental strength was destroyed.

The Eastern Front was now stabilised along a line which was to remain almost unchanged until the summer campaign unlocked it again. In the interim period the regiment underwent a great change in organisation when it was announced on 1 April 1942 that Grossdeutschland had been raised to the status of a division. A 2nd Grenadier Regiment was raised and postings and cross postings were the order of the day. When the new division settled down it prepared for the tasks which would lie ahead of it. Having suffered, endured and survived one winter on the Eastern Front the Grenadiers felt confident that they could meet and overcome any new challenge or demand which their enemy or their own High Command would make of them. In this confidence Infantry Division Grossdeutschland began to prepare for the forthcoming German summer offensive.

Four

Infantry Division Grossdeutschland:
The Eastern Front, 1942-43

The short history of 9th Panzer Division, *68 Kriegsmonate,* when dealing with the period of the fighting in which the Division was involved from the summer of 1942 to the spring of 1944 admits that the record suffers from certain defects. It regrets that the Corps War Diaries kept in Bundesarchiv's military records section in Freiburg do not give details of the sacrifice in the sub-units within the Corps establishment nor of the heroism on the part of those smaller commands which characterised the twenty months of battle.

This regrettable disadvantage is one which also affects the subsequent chapters of this book and the battles which are there described. As Grossdeutschland grew and changed its role we must, of necessity, move from the particular to the general and can no longer recount the actions of individual units as heretofore. It must be enough to detail the movements and actions of the Division, throwing the spotlight for a brief moment, and where the record demands it, on a particular detachment and recounting brief details of a specific and noteworthy battle in which it was engaged. Then, too, as the former sub-units of the original Grossdeutschland Infantry Regiment – the Führer Begleit and the others – expanded and themselves became major units when Grossdeutschland Division was amalgamated with the Brandenburg Division to form a Panzer Corps, then the actions of specific minor units are lost in the record of the whole.

In a unit where the men were as carefully selected as in Grossdeutschland in battles as fiercely fought as were those on the Eastern Front and in situations in which the human was crushed by the material it is distressing to consider what stories have to be left unrecounted. This is the bitterness in writing about an elite unit. The faces which stand out; the names which were synonymous with bravery and daring and for whose deeds there is no space here to recall. But more than the remembered names and the recognised faces are the unnamed and faceless men – the Grenadiers, fusiliers, musketeers, artillerymen, panzermen and others low in military rank but tall in sacrifice and dignity who advanced, withdrew, fought, bled, died, conquered or were defeated and for whom only books like this can serve as an epitaph.

The experiences of the first, disastrous winter of the war against the USSR had shocked both military and civilian Germany. The first year of the war had not fulfilled the expectations which had been raised that total victory would be achieved. The tactics used in former short and triumphal campaigns had failed to subdue the Soviet Union. For the first time in the war which had begun in September 1939 the German public heard that its Army had not merely been forced on to the defensive, but that it had been compelled to retreat. The objectives laid down for the three Army Groups had not been attained and a vast amount of territory which had been captured during the first, fast campaign had been lost during the winter. Only the men who had fought on the Eastern Front during these months of cold and misery could know the real depth of the bitterness of the defeat which had been inflicted or the agonies which had been suffered.

Nevertheless in the spring of 1942 troops of Army Group North still invested Leningrad; in the centre German pressure still menaced Moscow, while in the south German troops were in possession of the wealth of the Ukraine. Hitler's soldiers were hundreds of miles deep inside the Soviet Union and had carved out a vast territory rich in grain, coal and iron with which to nourish the German war machine. But, the Red Army had not been beaten in the field and was still a potent and unbroken force.

In that spring of 1942 the German planners were faced with problems which did not permit easy resolution. There was an awareness of the frightening strength of the Soviet military colossus and of their own weakness.

At OKW and OKH levels there was division and uncertainty about the course of action to be taken during 1942. Halder, at OKW, had no doubts at all: there should be no major campaign entered upon during that year. At best he proposed a series of limited offensives could be undertaken to erase salients and to 'tidy-up' the line. During this fallow year new equipment, above all new tank types, could be tested and produced in great numbers. The Army could be built up, re-equipped and retrained so that it would be capable of undertaking new and decisive battles during 1943.

Aware as Hitler was of the losses which the German Army had suffered, he still deluded himself that the Soviet losses had weakened the Red Army even more severely and his strategy for the forthcoming battles was based on that premise. He was prudent enough to appreciate that it was not possible for the German Army to launch a major assault against the whole length of the Soviet line and his decision was that only Army Group South would make the main effort.

Hitler's orders issued on 5 April outlined the main intentions of the summer campaign: the Soviet potential for prosecuting the war was to be seized by an advance to the oil fields of the Caucasus; the Red Armies in the south were to be destroyed west of the Don river; an advance was to be made into the region of Stalingrad firstly to encircle the Red Armies there and secondly to cover the northern Bank of the advance into the Caucasus. If 1941 can be given the description 'The year of Moscow', then 1942 must bear the fatal title 'The year of Stalingrad'. And yet no mention was made in the original operations order of the capture of the city on the Volga, only the area of Stalingrad was specified as a sector in which the Red Armies were to be trapped.

The grand assault by Army Group South would be made in a series of stages, each synchronised to begin as the preceding one ended and before each attack commenced there would be a concentration of the maximum strength at decisive points.

The strategic intention was to carry out encirclement blows. In the first of these the northern arm of the pincer formed by 1st and 4th Panzer Armies would break the Soviet front between the Don and the Donetz; the southern arm of the pincer would strike from the Volchansk area and a bridgehead would be established on the Don.

The opening phases would be chiefly infantry battles to breach the Soviet line through which the armour and motorised divisions would then pour to gain freedom of movement, drawing behind them strong infantry forces to consolidate the gains made. The opening attacks of the northern pincer were to thrust towards Voronezh and once the Don was reached and Army on the northern flank would form a defensive front covering the further advance by the armour south-eastwards down the west bank of the river. The task of maintaining the next stage of the offensive would then pass to 6th Army forming a smaller pincer arm and meeting that of 4th Panzer Army. Through this junction the Red Armies west of the Don would be encircled. The mass grouping of 6th Army and 4th Panzer Army would then strike down the banks of the Ukrainian river to link up with the third synchronised assault. In this 17th Army and 1st Panzer Army would have driven eastwards from the river Mius and then turn northwards to meet 4th Panzer and 6th Army coming down from the north encircling their Red Army's opponents. This host would then sweep, dividing in two main groups, towards their given objectives. The 4th Panzer and 6th Army would turn towards Stalingrad region to guard the northern flank of the advance into the oil bearing region of the Caucasus.

During all this time the manoeuvring armies would have to be protected against interference from the Soviet forces and the contingents supplied by Germany's allies had the task of forming a shield on the outer flank. The success of the summer offensive depended upon their fighting ability.

Thus far went the plan. Hitler's need to make Army Group South the most powerful of his three Groups drained off from the centre and north some of their best battle-hardened and well-equipped units. Thereby Army Group South was provided with nine of the nineteen panzer divisions at that time on the Eastern Front, with four of the ten motorised divisions available and with fifty-one of the total allied divisions which had been placed at Germany's disposal by the satellite governments. Thus 93 of the 189 divisions available were with Army Group South.

There were, however, qualifications which must be taken into account. The first of these was that very few of the German units were up to strength; the panzer divisions were so weak in armoured fighting vehicles that their actual strength was that of brigades and sometimes only of regiments. The second qualification was the combat efficiency of the satellite troops. Some were thoroughly dependable and well organised; but, taken as a whole, these contingents were an unbalanced collection armed with a miscellany of weapons and equipment.

Hitler, OKW and von Bock, the commander of Army Group South, were taking a calculated risk in depending upon the non-German divisions but this was a lesser risk than that of trying to push, with insufficient strength, on towards objectives vast distances removed from the start lines. The advances would be made in a region almost completely isolated by rail from the west and centre of the Soviet Union. The logistic problems facing the quatermaster's department were almost insoluble and added to the hazards were Soviet partisan bands whose increasing boldness during the campaign was to reduce considerably the flow of supplies to the forward troops. The last great factor in the whole equation was the unbeaten Red Army which stood with morale heightened, firm in the knowledge that it had held the Germans in the first year.

Before we go on to study the Soviet forces which were to take part in the great summer battles of 1942, let us state that there were now some new military voices at Stavka (Stavka Glavnovo Komandovaniya – Supreme Command Headquarters). It is the folly of civilians aspiring to be remembered as military commanders to issue orders that not an inch of territory be surrendered. The policy of Stalin and the old Bolshevik leaders at Kiev in the autumn of 1941, to name but one battle, had led to the loss of nearly one million Red Army soldiers. The new men in Stavka were quite prepared to give ground. Theirs was a policy of manoeuvre – not a fixed line of defence – of allowing the German enemy to over-stretch himself and then to cut off his head. Resistance would still be determined, even fanatical where it was required, but great battles of attrition were not the means by which Marshal Georgi K. Zhukov, General Ivan Koniev, Marshal Konstantin Rokossovski, General F.I. Tolbukhin and the other young commanders were determined to fight. It was the tragedy of the Red Army that although there were new ideas at staff command level the rigid patterns at combat level were precisely those which had occasioned the frightful losses in dead, wounded and captured which the Red Army had suffered during 1941.

Facing Army Group South were the Briansk Front which covered Moscow with its right wing and Voronezh with its left. The Voronezh area was held by the 40th Red Army. Through a lucky event Stavka was in possession of the complete German operational plan. A staff officer of 23rd Panzer Division had been shot down and these secret papers were found in his briefcase. Aware that the first and heaviest blow would come in the north, Stavka built up the strength of their forces around Voronezh, preparing for the counter-attacks which they would launch once the German assault lost impetus. To strengthen the defences along the Don two complete Armies and an armoured Army were placed in position. Thus facing the German left wing were no fewer than six Red Armies and it was against this mass of men, guns and tanks that the opening moves would be made.

Throughout the late spring reorganisations, troop movements and local offensives by both armies had been the features of life on the Eastern Front. A new excitement was in the air. It was campaigning time again. The front was being 'tidied up', salients pinched out, springboards for future operations were being gained. The battle line of Army Group

South which ran from Kursk southwards to Taganrog was being prepared for action and along its length the five armies on its establishment prepared to launch themselves successively against the Soviet Army. This summer of 1942 was to see a period of battle which opened with victorious advances and ended with the destruction of 6th Army, starved, frozen and held fast by Hitler's orders, in the ruins of Stalingrad.

That year of Stalingrad had run half its course when, on 28 June, 2nd Army struck the first blow. Then followed that of 4th Panzer Army. The advance towards the Don had begun and behind that river lay the mother river of the USSR – the Volga.

For the opening phases of the new offensive our concentration is upon 48th Panzer Corps of 4th Panzer Army, for it was with that Corps that Grossdeutschland Division, was to serve. The 48th Panzer Corps formed the extreme left wing of Army Group South and the tasks which had been assigned to it were to smash the Soviet line and race to the Don in a fast advance, to cut off the Red Army west of the great river and to destroy it there.

The history of the weeks which elapsed from the end of June 1942 to the middle of July is thus, so far as the Grossdeutschland Division is concerned, the story of the forcing of a breach, the penetration and exploitation of the situation and the attempts to attain the stated objectives. The distances to be covered were considerable; the enemy who had had time to construct elaborate and well-manned defences was strong and prepared, but once again the élan and superior tactics of the panzer men and the incredible marching ability of the German infantry brought short-lived victory to German arms.

During the evening of 27 June the codeword 'Siegfried' was flashed from 48th Corps signifying that its involvement in the summer offensive would commence on the following day.

Confident in their ability and with the full and certain knowledge of the great power which accompanied them the Grenadiers lay ready for the new offensive, although it was true that there had been no time for the division's component units to train or work together as a team. Both regiments had a common objective during the first phase; the Tim river.

From midnight gunfire flickered along the front as other corps moved forward towards their first objectives and these initial moves would, it was hoped, draw attention away from the rapid thrust which 48th Panzer Corps was to make.

The midsummer night of 27/28 June was short and before 03.00hr the sky had already begun to lighten but this paleness vanished in the brighter light of the shell bursts of a barrage which was poured on to the Soviet positions. At the height of this bombardment Stukas flying in from the still dark western sky roared overhead, their arrival coinciding with the infantry advance as the first files of Grenadiers went over the top and moved towards the smoke-shrouded Soviet lines.

Such had been the effect of the German barrage that at most places opposition was minimal or lacking altogether.

One battalion flung a company across the Tim river captured the bridge there and pushed forward to gain a bridgehead more than 2km deep on the eastern bank. Through this the reconnaissance battalion passed and pressed on to the Kshen river.

The foot march which other Grenadier battalions made lasted from dawn to dusk and the men trudged through the blazing heat of midsummer, beating off attacks by Red cavalry, advancing through artillery bombardments to form their own bridgehead on the Kshen.

Rain fell and produced mud holding the divisional transport so fast that it was not until 30th that the advance could be resumed. While overhead Stukas dive-bombed the Red armour the Grenadiers fought their way slowly through lines of trenches and strong points. The Red rearguard was making a stand and the fighting in which the men of Grossdeutschland were involved was made at close quarters chiefly with hand grenades and machine-pistols. Fighting was continuous as small groups of Grenadiers cleared one section of a trench system after the other: a hand grenade round a traverse and then a quick rush to capture a new piece of trench. To drive back those Soviet tanks which had escaped the dive-bombing Stukas, Grossdeutschland panzer battalion was brought forward and swept into the attack employing a shallow wedge formation so that each of its vehicles could engage the enemy. Coolly the individual tank commanders picked their targets and passed a stream of orders to their crews. This is a typical example of the fighting in which they were involved.

The turret began to swing and the operator pressed his eye to the optical sight. The gunner, his weapon loaded with armour-piercing shot, rotated the dial with his left hand to bring the enemy tank into focus thus giving the correct range. His right hand was just as busily engaged in working the elevating mechanism. Then as the target filled the optical sight he dropped his hand, took off the safety catch and awaited the order to fire. The concussion of the gun firing was lost in the excitement of seeing the T.34 burst open like an overripe fruit and then from the commander standing up in the turret came a change of target and the aimer searched for the new enemy. Another detonation; another enemy tank destroyed and then a jarring crash on the brow of the panzer where an anti-tank gun scored a direct hit which only the thick armour plate had prevented from being a complete penetration. The whole steppe was covered with burning vehicles and, with their aggressive move thwarted, the surviving Soviet tanks voided the field. The Grenadier advance was resumed on the regimental transports which had now arrived and into which the men embussed to push the advance forward at a faster pace eventually forming a salient against whose flanks Soviet armour and infantry assaults beat in unbroken succession.

One of the greatest features of German organisation during the war was the ease with which commanders could form battle groups. To speed the advance of the Grossdeutschland Division one such battle group was formed and its action must speak for all such ad hoc groups. It thrust its way across open country, through Soviet barrages under cover of which Red tanks moved down to intercept and to destroy the German unit. Undismayed at the array which faced them, the men of the group watched the Red armour approach and then deployed seeking the best defensive positions. Calmly the anti-tank gunners waited; the No. 1 with his eye trained on the approaching targets. The very ground vibrated from the detonation of explosions and from the rumbling tracks of the Soviet tanks but then came the order to return fire and within minutes seven of the advancing wave had been destroyed. Even though the Soviet commander switched the direction of his assaults from flank to flank he could not hold the Germans who had soon pushed on into Kulevska. Even there the Soviet counter-attacks went on and Red tanks fought against the German panzers and SPs in the narrow streets, Soon the village was dotted with smashed and burning vehicles from both armies. For a short while super heavy KV Is entered the battle but then the almost invincible 88mm flak guns were brought up and used as anti-tank weapons. Their high-velocity shells smashed the armour of several Soviet heavy tanks and drove back the remainder.

A breach had now forced in the Soviet line; the division expanded the gap and allowed the armour through but the Soviets had still not withdrawn completely and during the night of a July there were the unmistakable signs and sounds which indicated that they were building up their forces to undertake fresh counter-attacks of major dimensions.

When these came in they were little short of suicidal. Without pause, caring neither for wastage nor losses, four Soviet tank brigades were flung into battle between Kursk and Voronezh with the intention of halting the Grossdeutschland drive. But the German Corps commander had built an elaborate trap into which the furious Soviet tank advances were carefully channelled and at whose end were batteries of 88mm guns. Upon these the Soviets impaled their armoured fighting vehicles. In successive waves the Red armour poured froward, half hidden in the dust clouds thrown up by whirling tracks and the explosions of gun fire. Attacked from both flanks and halted by the gun line each Soviet charge was slowed, contained and flung back with heavy loss. Great numbers of tanks lay burning or shattered on the battlefield and this mass destruction of armour shattered the morale of the survivors. They retired in disorder. Then the race to the Don really began.

In their career the Grenadiers roared into, captured and left behind a succession of small hamlets and villages. It was not always and everywhere a glorious chase. Here and there the pell-mell drive was halted as groups of Soviet soldiers stood and fought to the death as, for example, at Krasnaya Polyana where only the use of flame throwers could crush the defence. By late in the evening the division had advanced more than 20km towards the Don and by 4 July the 4th Panzer Army had covered more than 160km.

The division's forward movement on the following morning was carried out by both panzer and soft-skinned vehicles which roared across the last kilometres separating Grossdeutschland from the river.

There the 2nd Regiment's task to seize the great railway bridge spanning the Don was unsuccessful for the spearhead units were too weak in number and by the time heavy weapons detachments had come up, the bridge was alight. The only way across the river now was by boat.

At midnight the Grenadiers slipped down the steep river bank, quickly embarked on to the rubber assault craft and paddled with muffled oars across the dark and slow-running stream. So great was the surprise of the silent operation and so successful its outcome that by dawn on 6 July two battalions had been established in a firm bridgehead.

The 1st Regiment's objective was a road bridge at Semiluki and it says much for the confidence of the German commanders in their men and the extent of the disruption to the Soviet opposition that only a single platoon was detailed to carry out reconnaissance and to clear a way forward along the 6km distance which separated the unit from the bridge. The swift thrust by the advanced guard entangled it on a number of occasions with a maelstrom of Red Army detachments and there were many times when the Grenadiers

The divisional SP battalion, 1943.

had to fight fierce little battles against a group of determined Soviet soldiers or a stubborn Soviet rearguard.

Not until last light did the platoon reach the bridge. A section ripped out the burning fuses of the detonating charges while the remainder flung themselves across the foot-way and established a perimeter. Against all expectations a small group of men had succeeded in forcing the Don and holding a tiny bridgehead. It was, however, one thing to obtain a perimeter but it was quite another to hold it until it could become a springboard for the advance upon Voronezh. It was then that the full extent of the trust and confidence between the *Luftwaffe* and the Grenadiers can be appreciated for Stukas came down and laid a bombing line to within 400m of the bridgehead group, softening up the Soviets and breaking up their counter-attacks.

The first SP guns were brought across to support the advance on Voranezh but both Grenadier regiments had been exhausted by the continuous fighting and all that could be achieved was a junction and amalgamation of their bridge-heads.

Voronezh fell to other troops and the first part of Hitler's strategic plan can be said to have been successfully completed. Not only had 4th Panzer Army torn a huge gap in the Soviet line between Kursk and Isiyum but it had linked with the 6th Army north-east of Valuiki. The success was qualified, however, by the fact that Stavka had withdrawn its forces across the Don. One of Hitler's intentions – to destroy the Red Army west of the river – had not been realised.

The point now arises whether the crossing of the Don by the German forces was a tactical error. It had not been the intention of the German Supreme Commander who placed a much greater emphasis on an advance down the Don so that when Hoth's divisions bounced the river the German leader's first impulse was to pull them back to the western flank. The evacuation by the Soviets of part of Voronezh influenced Hitler to allow a panzer advance on the city where the divisions were involved in a week-long battle during which the impetus of the drive south was lost and great inroads made upon the stocks of fuel which had been assembled for that purpose.

The descent down the Don began and Grossdeutschland which had been selected to add weight to the southward drive was relieved from the line and sent hurrying across the wide and open steppe, receiving road priority, forcing other units to move off the highway while the vehicles with the white painted German steel helmet tactical sign hurtled southwards.

The first day's drive covered 120km. Day followed day of long road marches allowing only a minimum of rest for men or vehicles. At times the columns outdistanced their supplies and the battle units were forced to halt for lack of fuel until the *Luftwaffe* dropped barrels of petrol by parachute from Ju52s. But the supplies brought by air were only a fraction of the division's requirements and enforced halts became more and more frequent. In this stop/start fashion more than 450km was covered, much of it without seeing a sign of the Soviet enemy. However, the troops on the line of communication – that perilously thin line which fed the spearpoint – were not so fortunate. Red Army units which were still withdrawing in good order to the river and who were unaware that in theory they had been cut off, clashed frequently and bloodily with the lightly armed men of the supply services.

New orders came from Corps: the division was to open its front and to descend upon several objectives, capturing these before going on to help encircle Soviet forces at Rostov. The lightning advance down the Don against only minimal opposition; the capture of Voroshilovgrad by 17th Army on 17 July and other successes had all convinced Hitler that there was now no obstacle to the implementation of the next part of his summer campaign.

On 9 July von Bock's command was divided into two groups. List had under his control Army Group A. Army Group B was under von Weichs. The objective for Army Group B was to reach Stalingrad and for Army Group A the oil of the Caucasus.

The Army Groups set out, each on its own mission, and the front they had to cover extended for over 2,000km. Such was the distance which separated them that when a setback occurred neither was near enough to help the other. There was no strategic reserve; everything had been committed.

During the second week of July the Grossdeutschland Division was still experiencing its stop/go operations and in order to keep the fighting vehicles moving petrol had been siphoned from the soft-skinned trucks and these, together with much of the infantry, had been left behind. Only the armoured heart of the division still carried on the advance. For one patrol mission the reconnaissance battalion drained dry the tanks of all vehicles save a handful and with this small group struck out to reach the Bystraya river. Orders still came in commanding a further advance southwards; on the 18th an order was received to press on to the Donets and during this operation a complete regiment of Soviet infantry was captured by a single Grenadier company of Grossdeutschland.

The very success of the Grossdeutschland drive contained dangers. The rapid advance had compressed the retreating Soviets and in their frantic efforts to escape German encirclement these launched attacks at the thin lines of German troops breaking through and overrunning the Grenadier lines wounding and killing mercilessly in their fierce determination to avoid capture. Along the line held by Grossdeutschland fire fights broke out as whole battalions of Red infantry flung themselves against isolated German companies and even single platoons.

Neither rockets, nor conventional artillery firing barrages of unprecedented fury, nor tank assault, nor yet the intervention of the Red Air Force could halt the division's resumed drive to the lower Don. For this mission a battle group of motor cyclists, anti-aircraft artillery and anti-tank guns was sent southwards to seize and hold any important features whose capture might facilitate the flow of the division's advance. Driving through the searing heat traversing a region notorious for its shortage of water but spending only the shortest time in rest and sleep, the group drove furiously until it reached the river. By 06.00 on 22 July the 1st Regiment had put 2nd Battalion across.

The speed of the Grossdeutschland's resumed advance had confused the Soviet defence and its defenders. Red Army men were taken prisoner and such masses of material that the advance guard could not even estimate it. Once the initial shock had passed, the Soviet Command offered desperate resistance to the German advance. This opposition was aided by the terrain of the lower Don which with its wide, shallow riverlets and soft, marshy ground afforded a natural obstacle to wheeled or tracked vehicles.

Back on the Don, Pioneers had erected a bridge and continued to shuttle units across the river in rubber assault boats. The advance must continue, the momentum must be kept up.

The Soviets, determined to resist in the naturally strong defensive country of the lower Don, put up opposition which involved the Grenadier companies in long and bitter fighting. Concealed in the undergrowth and with the patience of the hunter, infantrymen of the Red Army sniped at the Grenadier groups or else rose from the ground to storm forward and fight the German Grenadiers with rifle and bayonet, with entrenching tool or with knives. In such close fighting little quarter was asked or given; it was warfare at its most primitive – kill or be killed.

Not content merely to hold the Grenadiers in the dense forests, Stavka brought up strong reinforcements and in a sudden thrust struck forward to drive in the bridgehead but the German defence held firm and not only drove back the furious assaults but enlarged the perimeter out of which the Grenadiers advanced to the Mantych river.

There were times when it was only the shortage of petrol which held the Germans fast, and small detachments searched the area for Soviet fuel dumps, for collective farms in which supplies might be kept and by such ad hoc methods managed to maintain the furious pace of the chase.

Then on 1 August came more welcome news. The division was to form part of OKH

Reserve and the regiments pulled back across the Don.

While on its own sector Grossdeutschland had been fighting its way forward, pressure along the rest of the line of Army Group South had also been maintained. On 1 August Army Group A crossed the Kuban river and the assaulting divisions split up to carry out their allotted tasks in the great plan. Pyatigorsk, near the Caspian Sea, fell to 1st Panzer Army; its tanks reached the Tireh river and threatened the oil fields at Grozny. The situation facing the Red Army was a serious, even desperate one. Its defence operations between 28 June and 24 July both in the area of Voronezh and in the Don bend had been unsuccessful and it had had to undertake a withdrawal of between 150 and 400km.

The Soviets had failed to hold the German assault, and had lost to a foe numerically inferior to themselves the whole of the Ukraine and the industrial Donetz bend, while the rich agricultural area of Kuban and the oil fields at Maikop were under threat. Army Group B was making its way slowly towards Stalingrad and by 23 August was within 40 km of the great bend in the Volga south of the city.

The great and substantial successes achieved by the Germans contained dangers. Between the northern and the southern Army Group there yawned a vast distance and not all that great arc could be held in strength; some of it was not garrisoned at all. The four hundred kilometres between the Volga and the Terek were undefended. Where there were troops the greatest number of the divisions holding the line were the units of the satellite states. Many of these, lacking transport, were moving on foot from their concentration areas and until they took up position in the battle line, German formations, whose strength might have added to the thrusts towards Stalingrad or towards the Caucasus, were held fast.

Then, too, there was the Red Army. Although forced back across the Don and then back towards the Volga its commanders did not lose heart but were determined to regain the military initiative. The turning point came for them with Order No. 227 dated 28 July. The gist of this was that the German enemy had reached far enough and for the future there was to be 'not a step back'.

This uncompromising command rallied the Red Army and during the fighting which flared in the autumn and burnt throughout the Soviet winter offensive, two towns, in addition to that of Stalingrad, achieved a prominence and a notoriety for the bitterness of the fighting which was carried on around them. These towns are Voronezh and Rzhev. Both had fallen to the Germans during the opening phases of the summer offensive and were vital to the war plans of Stavka who ordered them to be recaptured, cost what it might. This simple order brought new battles of attrition during which thousands upon thousands were to be killed or wounded and hundreds of thousands were to suffer the bitter privation of a second winter.

The fighting around Rzhev, summer and autumn 1942

The summer sun was pleasant and for the men of the Infantry Division Grossdeutschland there was now time to forge with the newly joined reinforcements those bonds of comradeship which are the most enduring memory of the front line soldier and which are the strength of a combat unit. An infantry soldier is seldom unaware that the time will come when some demand will be made upon him and for the Grenadiers this time was not far removed. The area in which they were next to fight was Rzhev and the battles in which they were to be engaged were to occasion them heavy and bitter losses.

The importance of Rzhev to the battle plans of both armies cannot be too greatly stressed. Rzhev to the north, like Voronezh to the south, was a springboard for any German advance upon Moscow. In like fashion both were springboards for Soviet plans aimed at the encirclement of Army Group Centre or the outflanking of either Army Group South or North. For the future development of Soviet strategy the possession of these places was essential and the failure to recapture Rzhev during the great winter offensive of 1941-2 had been a severe setback to Stavka plans. Now, in the autumn of 1942, Voronezh had fallen to the Germans. Stavka strengthened the front around the town to halt any further German advance towards the capital while it prepared for an assault which would recapture the northern bastion, Rzhev.

In one sense Stavka had miscalculated. The main German military effort during the summer offensive of 1942 had been towards the Caucasus and the seizure of Voronezh had not been planned. With the main effort of the summer offensive undertaken by Army Group South neither of the other Groups had any immediate tasks and the commander of Army Group Centre therefore cleaned up the pockets of resistance which had been left after the Soviet winter offensive. In those months Lieutenant-General Walther Model, 9th Army Commander, had taken part in this tidying-up operation near Rzhev during which he had destroyed one Red Army and a cavalry corps as well as shattering two other Armies. Then the emphasis had swung away from Rzhev.

When the tidying-up operation on its front had been completed, 9th Army formed a salient whose base was Rzhev. Soviet attempts were then made to seize the town or to reduce the salient for its capture would not only cut off the whole of 9th Army but the greater part of 4th Army as well. Throughout the early summer the Soviet High Command drew together forces in order to undertake a pincer attack upon the salient and the troops of 30th Army were to strike from the north aiming to seize the town while from the east First Red Army with 29th Army in support would drive in to cut the railway and thereby to isolate the troops at the point of the salient from those in its base.

On 27 July Koniev, the Front Commander, issued orders for the assault and intimated that whatever the loss Rzhev must be taken. The suffering and the effort were to be in vain for despite the bitterest fighting Rzhev remained in German hands.

Slowly at first but then with increasing rapidity 30th Red Army struck down from the north hoping by frontal assault to bludgeon its way to a quick victory. Then from the east the other Armies drove in and within days the battle reached the first of the climaxes which marked its progress. Bowing to the pressure of the Soviet assaults Model drew back his outpost line across the Volga.

The size, direction and force of the main Soviet assault had been severely underestimated but once this had been established three panzer and a number of infantry divisions of which Grossdeutschland was one were alerted and moved into the salient with orders to hold Rzhev at all costs.

The main Soviet drive brought troops of First Army into a small town at the confluence of the Vasuga and Volga rivers where they established a bridgehead and threatened to cut the vital railway line. To halt the Red flood would be the task of the Grossdeutschland Division and the other formations which had been brought into the salient.

At the beginning of September aerial reconnaissance showed that the Soviets were massing for a major attack intended to produce the victory which had thus far eluded them. D-Day for the opening of this new Soviet assault was 9 September.

The barrage which opened at dawn that day was of an intensity equalling only the major bombardments of the First World War and behind the curtain of shells came the assault infantry; wave after wave moving forward on a narrow front and almost shoulder to shoulder, so great was their number. The force of their attack pushed back the German front line producing a local crisis which caused Grossdeutschland to be put on two hours' notice to move.

The division's tasks were to fling back the Soviet incursions and to regain the former front line. Their attack was to go in at dawn on the following day.

The first lines of the Grossdeutschland companies emerged from the woods through which they had made their approach march and into the view of Soviet artillery observers who then directed upon them every available artillery piece, hoping by cannonade to destroy the assault before it could shake out. Wave after wave of fighter bombers strafed the advancing troops with anti-personnel bombs. The Red Armies were determined to crush the attack.

The Grossdeutschland infantry line vanished completely in smoke and dust as the artillery began to smash the cohesion of the attack. The gun smoke drifted away and there could be seen advancing through the shell-bursts groups of infantry fewer in number than before the barrage but still maintaining the momentum of the advance. Soviet armoured fighting vehicles drove in against the German infantry, but roaring from behind the crest over which the Grenadiers had advanced the Grossdeutschland Panzer Battalion swept down upon the Soviet tanks. The artillery fire of three Red Army corps was now concentrated upon the German infantry and armour and soon black smoke clouds showed where the Soviet guns had hit and smashed a panzer. Losses began to mount.

The lie of the land forced the panzer to advance along avenues which the Soviet gunners covered with heavy and accurate fire. The tank companies had also begun to suffer losses from the fields of green coloured mines which blended so well with the grass of the marsh. Every step of the assault, every turn of the tracks brought the Grenadiers and the panzer men closer to that point in the attack when losses become too high and the first signs of nervousness, presaging a withdrawal become evident. In this assault there could be no such hesitation; no shirking from the responsibility which was theirs. The fate of 9th Army rested upon the success of this attack. Grossdeutschland had been selected to carry it out because there were no better troops than they; no soldiers in the German Army more able than those who carried on their right cuff the title of their allegiance.

But there comes a time when flesh and blood can no longer stand against a material superiority. The advance began to slow and neither regiment reached its given objective. There was a short pause to regroup, and a new advance was ordered – but it was in vain. The frustration which may have been felt could be tempered with the knowledge that although the division had failed to restore the old front line it had halted the forward movement of one Red Army infantry and an armoured corps.

At last light both regiments consolidated and the roll was called. The losses were frightening. From one platoon which went into the attack with forty-two men, only sixteen had survived. Other companies and battalions had suffered nearly as great a proportion of losses.

The dawn of 11 September brought the resumption of the Grossdeutschland Grenadiers' advance against sixty massed batteries of Soviet artillery which swamped the vehicles of the panzer battalion with fire as they reached Suchtino.

The Soviets massed more batteries of artillery to support their own infantry and tank attack against the Grossdeutschland line. But for the regiments of Grossdeutschland the order was to continue the assault. In front of the small groups of men, reduced by the brutal losses of the previous day, a wall of black earth rose into the air as shells exploded from heavy and light artillery pushed into the Red infantry's front line positions and the multi-barrelled Stalin organ rockets. The air was alive with whirring shrapnel and bullets as from the flanks of the advance, Soviet snipers picked off the Grenadiers struggling through the bombardment. 'Oh, God let it be dark,' must have been the fervent prayer of many of those facing the fury of that destructive fire.

Then at 02.00hr on 12th came the first of the Soviet counter-attacks which were to form the main part of the drama of the following days and now, faced with an enemy at whom they could hit back, the Grenadiers exacted a fearful loss from the mass of Red Army infantry charging towards them and swept the Soviet battalions from the field. Throughout the night the living advanced across the dead and as hour succeeded hour the assaults became weaker until the final one at 16.00 was crushed almost as soon as it had crossed its start line. The area in front of the Grossdeutschland positions had been turned into a cratered landscape thickly sown with the bodies of the dead. This had been no battle, but a slaughter and the Soviet infantry had paid the price which Koniev had said was acceptable; but it had all been in vain, no penetration of the German line had been made.

The Grenadiers were incapable of bringing the advance forward and the next days were spent in consolidating positions. Then on 15 September, the first of another series of Soviet armoured assaults came in at 07.00hr. The Red tanks were swept back by the fire of the division's artillery and by the SPs and panzers which lay waiting for them in ambush positions.

Rain and mud halted operations on the divisional sector and both sides took advantage of the relative calm to regroup.

For the Germans the fighting then took on more and more the character of positional warfare with local attacks and the monotonous daily grind of survival against an enemy superior in artillery, tanks and men.

Soaked by rain, isolated in the thick mists of the swamps, shivering in the cold, existing on rations which were reduced again and again, the Grenadiers of the Grossdeutschland Division stayed in their crumbling trenches deeply aware that the losses within their companies meant that their numbers would soon be too few to hold back the Soviet storm.

A new operation was ordered for 30 September to establish a firm front line and every man who could bear arms was taken from the non-fighting echelons. In this attack the soldiers of the rear echelons, unskilled in infantry combat fell in batches, victims of the Soviet barrages or of the infantry assaults when the Soviet counter-attacks came in against them.

The enemy batteries fired with a furious speed as the Grenadiers stormed into the Soviet trenches bombarding friend and foe indiscriminately. The two forces were now so closely entangled that even hand grenades were too dangerous to use and then it was entrenching tools with sharpened edges and the mutilated wounded trampled in the mud of the trench floor. The Staff Officers at HQ had had their attack and the toll proved to have been excessive. At best a few hundred yards were gained, but so great were the losses that Grossdeutschland had been reduced to the strength of a single weak regiment.

Slowly the intensity of fighting died away and on 2 October came the announcement that the titles of the infantry regiments of the Grossdeutschland Division were to be changed and that 1st Regiment would be known as the Grenadier Regiment and 2nd as the Fusilier Regiment. Of greater significance was the announcement of a move back into reserve.

Rzhev had held, thanks to the staunch defence which had been maintained by the Division and all the men who had served there. The war continued and now ahead of them all loomed the spectre of another winter in the USSR and the certainty of the new major Soviet offensive.

The Soviet winter offensive and Manstein's counter-attack

Towards the end of October 1942 the fighting for Rzhev flared up again and in the ensuing combat the Grossdeutschland Division, acting as a counter-attack reserve force, had its component formations split among a number of divisions.

Not every unit in an army has the same capabilities. Some are better in attack than in defence, others can accept a loss rate which would render another impotent. One cannot, therefore, judge too harshly the 86th Infantry Division whose collapse was responsible for Grossdeutschland Division enduring a period of such shocking misery that survivors of that bitter bloodletting recall its horrors only with deepest reluctance. The sober unemotional words in the war diaries do not betray very much of the horrors endured in that passage of the division through the period of one of its greatest crises – the battle of the Luchessa river valley.

This was carried out for much of the time at a period when the first, heavy snow storms reduced visibility, when sudden thaws produced the *rasputitsa* (cloying mud) and in badly sited and unprepared positions. Stavka had co-ordinated its thrusts to destroy the Rzhev salient and pressure was simultaneously applied against the eastern and western walls of the salient. The Grossdeutschland front faced generally west and then north-westwards against two Soviet tank corps whose task it was to thrust along the valley and to cut the main Byelo/Olenin road while, attacking on the eastern side of the salient other Red Army units strove to cut the vital railway.

When the 86th Division collapsed only one Grossdeutschland unit was uncommitted to battle and, against the 21,000 Red Army soldiers who were driving into the German defences, Model sent in 2nd Battalion of the Grenadier Regiment, his last reserve, to hold a line which an ordinary division had failed to maintain. The Grenadier battalion stood in this breach, isolated and with its flanks unprotected while towards and round it roared waves of Red Army infantry and tanks.

Battle patrols fought back the storming Soviet thrusts and the Grenadiers extended their hold until eventually a thin line extended across the valley of the Luchessa. Then, further Grossdeutschland units became free and were moved in to thicken the line; but they were still too few in number to relieve the Grenadiers who in water-logged or snow-filled slit trenches, soaked through, and frequently without any food, still held on. Their life in the line was a time of unprecedented strain. For hours a barrage would crash down upon the slit trenches; a lull, a pause in the bombardment, the shouts from slit trench to slit trench to see who had survived, a cry for stretcher bearers and then as nerves began to feel less taut would come the whizz-bang bombardment as the orchestrated concert of artillery resumed. Then there would be a sudden silence as the barrage ended. The incautious soldier who poked his head out now above the edge of the slit trench would fall back dead, victim of one of the snipers who had infiltrated and who lay concealed behind one of the Soviet dead or hidden in a burnt-out tank hulk.

Then the Grenadiers listened to hear whether there was the throaty bellow which indicated an infantry assault or the reverberating thunder of Otto tank engines as the T.34s warmed up ready to make yet another attempt to destroy this block in their path. The infantry attack was the easier to defeat even though the Red infantry formed solid blocks of men into whose huge brown mass fire was poured, seemingly without effect, until at last they recoiled and swept back ignoring the commissars' pistols, seeking refuge from the bullets of those seemingly indestructible Germans, who now only two battalions strong, were frustrating the efforts of two tank corps.

Brutal assaults against a unit on the flank of the Grossdeutschland line punched a hole through which roared Red infantry and tanks which then struck the Grossdeutschland battalions in the back. Between the Soviet forces pounding from the west and the east there was a thin line of Grenadiers without the weapons capable of destroying the newer Soviet heavy tanks whose battalions came roaring in. The German 50mm Pak was ineffective against Soviet armour, except at point blank range and where there were no captured Soviet 76.2mm guns to turn against their former owners then squads of tank hunters went out to attack the steel monsters with satchels of explosive.

The battle reached its climax as the Soviets threw in every available man to smash the Grenadiers and the first day of December marked the high tide of the Soviet effort when three Soviet infantry divisions went into the assault behind waves of tanks. The Grenadier line was forced back again and again until at last, overstretched by days of battle it broke and allowed the T.34s to sweep forward and to threaten the vital road.

The German line reformed a little further back still under tremendous pressure but the Grenadiers were winning a defensive victory. On 2 December there was a slight, but perceptible lessening in the Soviet drive, even though they had now reached to within two kilometres of the road.

But now other German units had been brought in and, now with their back well guarded, the Grenadiers flung themselves at every Soviet assault calling down Stukas to their aid. The defence had held. 120 Red tanks lay smashed in the Luchessa valley. The pace of the attacks died down as the Soviets began pulling back. Immediately Grossdeutschland swung into counter-attack and those companies which had borne the burden of the past weeks' fighting were withdrawn from action.

Pockets of Soviet infantry were attacked as the battalions 'tidied-up' the battlefield. Then on 22 December the Soviets again went over to the assault against the Fusilier Regiment as it moved forward through snow and thick fog.

After Christmas the Division attacked north of the Luchessa river, was involved in a limited operation during 30 December and still pushing slowly northwards captured Merkushy. That town was intended to form a main defensive position in the fortifications which were to be constructed to guard the salient. On 9 January 1943 Grossdeutschland passed into Reserve. An old German military proverb talks of the Regiment 'which dies in battle ten times, and is ten times reborn to remain – the Regiment'.

Not ten times yet, but already more than once the regiments of the Infantry Division Grossdeutschland had been reborn and then in the battles which would be fought in the Soviet winter offensive they were to suffer a bloodletting as grievous as that which they had undergone in the Luchessa valley.

During the time that the Infantry Division Grossdeutschland was fighting in the Luchessa valley 6th German Army had been totally destroyed in the agony of Stalingrad.

When Grossdeutschland entered the line again on 22 January the men had the feeling that they were moving into a military vacuum for during their patrols they had seen almost no other German troops. The advance to contact ended during 23rd when the first Soviet thrusts were met along a defensive zone along which mobile counter-attack forces were positioned. There was no dependence upon the satellite units holding the front on either flank of the division for these were in full flight, pursued by Soviet armoured columns or harried along the line of their retreat by Cossacks who sabred the scattered groups of infantry.

In the middle of this mass were Grossdeutschland standing firm while past it and heading westward, poured the shattered Italian, Romanian and Hungarian formations. Slowly the Grossdeutschland Division and its neighbouring SS unit Das Reich formed a cohesive front in and around Oskol.

Through the crumbling German front Soviet tank spearheads thrust forward gaining as much ground as they could before the spring thaw halted the advance or before the great Soviet offensive ran out of steam. Through the German front they roared; behind the positions still being held; to roll them up, outflank them and cut off their garrisons.

With an ever increasing speed the situation which had been serious deteriorated to become critical as the Red armour struck for Byelgorod. A Grenadier battalion formed a cordon to the north of the town to hold the mass tank assaults which came in on 8 February from the north and the north-east. Street fighting marked the passage of the Grossdeutschland Grenadiers as they fought and were driven from the burning town, and the units withdrew, leapfrogging to bring themselves back into the main German battle line. On the evening of 13th, the tired and exhausted Grenadiers entered the northern outskirts of Kharkov, but even there found no respite as Red Army troops who had infiltrated into the chaos of the capital forced the Grenadiers to fight savage street battles.

Kharkov presented a dismal spectacle to the combat soldier. Along its wide streets columns of rear echelon formations were jammed, all hoping to have escaped from the city before the Soviet armour had encircled it. Soviet citizens who could expect neither justice nor mercy from the execution squads of the NKVD (*Narodnaya Kommissiya Vnutrennix Dyel* or People's Commission for Internal Affairs), were also heading out of town; looting was rife, panic was everywhere, the whole front was in dissolution.

The possession of Kharkov was now central to the plans of the dictators who directed the opposing armies. Both saw in its possession a propaganda success and each was determined to gain this morale-boosting victory whatever the long-term military consequences might be. Thus Hitler sent a string of orders demanding that the town be held at all costs, while Stalin sent spearheads careering past the southern outskirts of the town, infiltrating his forces through the northern suburbs. By the evening of 15 February the situation was critical for the troops still in Kharkov as armoured pincers were flung around it.

Grossdeutschland had prepared to move out of the dying city but, in the face of Hitler's order again took up their positions. The division was compressed into a tight perimeter, holding an escape route under heavy pressure from Soviet troops who were determined to close this exit.

General Paul Hausser, the commander of the SS troops in Kharkov, was in a difficult situation for the SS had sworn unconditional loyalty to Hitler and the Führer's order had been unmistakably clear – the city would be held to the last. On the other hand military sense demanded an immediate evacuation, for to stay would invite the inevitable and rapid destruction of some of the finest German units in the Army Group.

Hausser listened to a plan by Manstein in which ground would be given up until the Soviet drive over-reached itself whereupon the revived German counter-punch would strike. Hausser ordered the evacuation of Kharkov and Grossdeutschland began its move out of the city at 16.00hr down the narrow corridor, less than a kilometre wide, along which the German garrison retreated.

The Soviet troops pressed their pursuit and the retreating SS Corps and the Grossdeutschland each took its turn as rearguard halting to face the onrushing waves of Soviet armour

One Red Army assault which came in during the bitterly cold night of 18 February struck and over-rolled the remnants of a Grenadier company. No survivor returned to the battalion positions from those men who, shivering with cold, hungry, outnumbered and exhausted, had held the wall of snow which had formed their forward defence line. On 19th the Grossdeutschland Division was ordered to collaborate with the SS in an attack, but under Soviet pressure this was cancelled and indeed the hope of forming a firm front was jeopardised by the collapse of a unit on Grossdeutschland's flank.

Stavka continued to thrust its armies headlong into the trap which had been laid at Kharkov. Manstein had been informed of the increasing exhaustion of the Soviet combat troops and had judged his moment carefully. As the Soviet columns halted to regroup he flung in 4th Army, aiming to close the gaps in the German front and to decapitate the Red tank spearheads. This masterly counter-attack destroyed two Red armies and in a swinging drive regained in some sectors that old battle line from which the Germans had been driven in the opening moves of the Red offensive. Grossdeutschland left the line, was reinforced, rested and re-equipped. The fire power of the whole division was being increased and even Tiger tanks were issued to the heavy tank battalion.

The short days of rest were soon over and the division took part in the Byelgorod operation.

At dawn on 7 March, following behind a short but intense barrage, the columns swung into action striking the surprised Soviet enemy, compelling him to a hasty withdrawal and to abandon masses of equipment. The days of the *blitzkrieg's* glorious advances had returned and the Grossdeutschland armour drove forward, over-running Red Army units trying to escape from these bitter soldiers who had changed from being the hunted and the chased to become the hunters and destroyers. The panzers led by Colonel Hyazinth von Strachwitz, Germany's finest tactical commander, roared through the retreating Red armour like a white-hot lance; over-rolling the Pak before it could be formed into fronts and turning the disciplined bodies of Soviet infantry into cowed and beaten men.

Soviet losses in armoured fighting vehicles were frightful and whole squadrons were sacrificed to gain time for the main body to reform. The conduct of the fighting had swung in favour of the thrusting Grossdeutschland whose attacks gained so much ground that the division once again formed a salient. Against this Red Army forces which had been assembled to strike at Kharkov, now had to be redeployed and it was against this more dangerous thrust that Stavka concentrated. Grossdeutschland Division made aware from reconnaissance reports of the build-up of the Soviet force on its sector regrouped ready to engage it.

For the next three days a furious and almost incessant tank battle was fought out at the approaches to Byelgorod. One column alone which roared into the fight against the panzer battalions of the Grossdeutschland Division held no fewer than one hundred and twenty T.34s. The artillery waited; the gunners immobile beside their weapons. There was a slight rise over which, like a modern cavalry charge the Soviet vehicles poured and presented for a moment their less heavily armoured under surfaces. Six T.34s blew up or caught alight in that first salvo and those which survived the destructive cannonade were fired at by panzers in hull down positions. A total of forty-eight Soviet tanks were destroyed on that sector during that first day and the Fusiliers attacked and forced to withdraw the Red infantry moving with the tank columns. Heavy tank attacks on 20th were repelled and a further twenty-eight Soviet machines were shot to pieces while on another flank the 1st Panzer Battalion killed another thirty-four Soviet armoured fighting vehicles. The successes of the past days were proclaimed in the OKW communiqué which announced that Grossdeutschland had smashed three Soviet infantry divisions and two anti-tank brigades which had sought to impede its advance. The Grossdeutschland infantry and panzer men continued their battle until they had reached and crossed the Kharkov/Byelgorod road. The division was taken out of the line.

During the months that Grossdeutschland Division was to remain out of the line reorganisations and new weapon scales gave indications that there was to be an upgrading of the divisional status and on 23 June 1943 it was proclaimed as an Order that Grossdeutschland would be from that date a Panzer Grenadier Division.

Among the changes was an increase to three in the number of its panzer battalions, the raising of a fourth battalion of artillery, the expansion of the flak units to six battalions, and the conveyance of 1st Battalion of the Grenadier Regiment in armoured personnel carriers – the same type of vehicle in which the Engineers 1st Battalion was also carried. To protect the divisional headquarters a defence company was raised and a counter-attack unit was formed to be at permanent readiness.

The division filled out with men and, with its weapons and vehicles, establishments at full strength could look forward with confidence to the battles which would await it during those months of 1943 which lay ahead.

Senior commanders of the German Army at Potsdam Parade.

German Infantrymen fighting through a railway siding.

Fieseler Storch aircraft waiting to take off on 12 May 1940.

Two Fieseler Storch aircraft which took part in Operation Nivi.

The infantry attack opens up in Eastern Poland during Operation Barbarossa.

Men of the Infantry Regiment Grossdeutschland halt for a rest.

A machine gun group with an MG 34.

An MG 34 group in house-to-house fighting.

The summer offensive of 1942.

The landscape of the Ukraine during the summer campaign of 1942.

An MG 34 in action as a heavy machine gun during the winter of 1942/43.

German infantry in a Soviet street during the 1942 summer offensive.

A flame thrower group of Grossdeutschland Panzer Grenadier Division.

Infantry and self-propelled guns move forward into an attack.

An SP on a Panzer III chassis, with an FOO on a rear housing.

The panzers move forward during the summer offensive of 1943.

The effect of a direct hit by am 88mm shell.

A machine gun group move up late in 1944 in East Prussia.

A Panzer V (Panther) in action during the fierce fighting south-west of Königsberg.

An SdKfz 251/1 in action during the fighting in East Prussia, autumn 1944.

The face of the German soldier after the hard fighting during the 1942 summer campaign.

The Panzer V Panther.

The 75mm PAK 41.

The hollow charge; the first effective weapon against tanks at close quarters.

Colonel *Hyazinth von Strachwitz.*

Tanks and infantry moving together, France 1940.

Armoured troop carriers with Panzer Grenadiers, Southern Russia, 1941.

Panzers push into Russia, 1941.

Panzer tank (PzKpfw II), Russia, 1942.

A PzKpfw IV, Russia 1942.

PzKpfw IV, Russian Steppes, 1942.

Tank commander checks advance positions with a commander of the Panzer Grenadiers, Russia, 1942.

Commanders take a rest, Kharkov, 1943.

The panzer divisions approach Kharkov, 1943.

The Red Square in the damaged town of Kharkov, March 1943.

Tanks forming up prior to Operation Citadel, Russia July 1943.

A tank commander prepares for Operation Citadel, *July 1943.*

A PzKpfw IV with armoured turret, Russia 1943.

Generaloberst *Heinz Guderian, Commander of Panzer Group II.*

Generaloberst *Hoth, Commander of Panzer Group III, with his Chief of Staff,* Oberst *Freiherr von Hünersdorf.*

Five

Panzer Grenadier Division Grossdeutschland: The Eastern Front, 1943-44

During the period from the summer of 1943 to the autumn of 1944 the military position on the Eastern Front was revolutionised when, after July 1943, the military initiative was wrested from the Germans. By the end of that year their situation had so deteriorated that strategically they were forced on to the defensive and under the successive blows of the aggressive Red Army had been pushed back further and further from the lands which they had conquered in the campaigns of the first two years. Then in the late summer of 1944 a Soviet offensive opened in Byelo Russia. Its force shattered Army Group Centre and this collapse compelled Hitler to undertake unforeseen and major troop movements to seal the shattered front. It was not so much these ad hoc methods which brought the brilliantly conducted offensive to a temporary halt; rather more it was the fact that the Soviet spearheads had outrun their supply systems.

We are here first concerned with the German offensive around Kursk in July 1943 which has passed into military history as Operation Citadel and whose outcome brought about this change of roles on the Eastern Front. The Soviet victory in the Kursk salient was a battle which was decided in less than a week although the fighting lasted for several months. Within those few short days the fate of the German Army of the Eastern Front was sealed; henceforth it would be the anvil to be struck by the Soviet hammer.

The time spent by the Panzer Grenadier Division Grossdeutschland in the Kursk offensive was not of long duration but in order that the course of the battles which it fought there is understood some brief details of the background to the offensive must be given.

The result of the Soviet winter offensive, whose end had been hastened by Manstein's victory at Kharkov, was that there existed a vast, Soviet salient some 150km deep and about 100km wide pressing into the inner flanks of Army Groups South and Centre. By early summer 1943 the Red Army, now at its peak strength of 500 divisions, was ready to resume its interrupted onslaught. Stavka decided, however, to let the Germans strike first, to absorb that blow and then to riposte with a counter-thrust once the whole German reserve had been committed.

Operation Citadel: *The Battle of Kursk, July 1943*

The one overriding question at Hitler's headquarters was what was to be the objective of the 1943 summer offensive? If there had to be an offensive then this must be undertaken to reduce the Kursk salient. Many of the senior German commanders in the field asked that the operation be undertaken without delay once the ground had hardened, otherwise Soviet power would continue to grow until it became immovable. Other commanders were completely against the plan. Once Kursk had been agreed as the objective plans were drawn up but the hesitance of the Supreme Commander postponed the opening of the operation. Hitler was aware that the Soviet forces in the salient were being built up and that his choices were reduced to two. Unless he attacked quickly Soviet strength would be so great that it would burst out of the confines of the bulge which pressed into the German positions. Kursk would thus have become a springboard for the Soviets. Alternatively, should the Soviets decide to remain on the defensive the longer the Germans delayed their own attack the more time would be given to the Soviets to strengthen the defences inside the salient.

Having decided on the place there then arose the question of how the salient was to be taken out. Hitler's plan was the classic pincer operation; from the north and south both jaws heading to meet at a point east of Kursk.

The maximum German effort was to be made by the southern pincer arm and the main combat force of Army Group South during this coming offensive was to be Colonel-General Hermann Hoth's 4th Panzer Army. A simultaneous but weaker thrust would be made by Army Group Centre's 9th Army commanded by Model.

Hitler knew he must succeed if he were to retain operational freedom and he promised his commanders vast numbers of men and material, assuring them that they would have qualitative superiority in the new armoured fighting vehicles which were being produced. The most important of these new weapons was the Panzer V – the Panther – and Hitler placed such dependence upon this tank that he cancelled D-Day for the offensive on several occasions because insufficient numbers had been produced. Even by the end of May the total in service was still fewer than 100 and when, eventually, sufficient had been produced they were set on their march to the front. No fewer than a quarter of the 204 vehicles fell out. Many of these non-starters were the victims of the early-type Panther's chief defect, a fault in the cooling system, which frequently caused the engine to catch fire.

Whether, indeed, the German tanks were qualitatively superior is open to doubt, but quantitively the Wehrmacht was inferior in every arm. All writers on the battle agree that about four million men were involved in the fighting and Koniev has estimated that the strength of the German forces at the opening of the offensive rose from 900,000 to 950,000. His estimates of German strengths include 10,000 artillery pieces and 2,700 armoured fighting vehicles of which 1,137 were with the southern pincer.

The 4th Panzer Army, the strike force of Army Group South, was grouped along a 50km front. On the left flank was its own assault group, 84th Panzer Corps, with II SS Panzer Corps in the centre of the line and with 3rd Panzer Corps on the right wing. For its vital part in the forthcoming operation, 84th Panzer Corps was given three elite divisions: 3rd and 11th Panzer and the Panzer Grenadier Division Grossdeutschland out of the total of ten panzer, one panzer grenadier and seven infantry divisions which made up the establishment of 4th Panzer Army. The greatest number of the new Panthers and Tigers were with the assault divisions.

Army Group South issued its operation orders. The task of 4th Panzer Army was to strike west of Byelgorod and to move via Oboyan, some 50km distance from the start line on to Kursk.

Against the German build-up the Soviets placed two complete Fronts – the Voronezh and the Central – and channelled to the divisions of the eleven armies positioned inside the salient every available man and tank until the whole bulge was filled with 40 per cent of the Red Army's foot and armour strength. The first line of Vatutin's Voronezh Front, holding the south, was held by 38th, 47th, 6th and 7th Guards Armies. In his second line was 1st Tank Army, 69th Army and, further back in reserve, a group of three Army Corps. Along the sector held by one army a total of 59,032 anti-tank and 70,994 anti-personnel mines had been laid, while the density of guns and mortars was 35 per kilometre. The superiority vis à vis the Germans on the Voronezh Front was 2:1 in infantry, 4:1 in artillery and 1.5:1 in armour.

As an example of the depth and development of the defences on the right wing of Rokossovski's Central Front these had reached a depth of between 30-35km by 4 July, and in 13th Army sector, for example, 'there were thirteen anti-tank areas (Pak fronts) incorporating forty-four strong points, in the main line…nine areas with thirty-four strong points in the second line and fifteen areas with sixty strong points in the third line.' Defences of this depth and intricacy had been built round the walls of the salient during the months of waiting and preparation.

The Soviet defence plans were based upon a complete knowledge of Hitler's plan through a cell of agents at OKW level and confirmed by their own excellent Intelligence network. Only in one respect were they deceived; they had expected the main blow to be struck by the northern pincer and had thus deployed the greatest part of their vast strength there. Whatever anxieties Stavka may have had about the course of the battle they knew that the German Army of 1943 was not the host which had attacked them in 1941. They were also aware of how much they themselves had learned and of their own strength. In tank production, for example, their production had risen to 30,000 tanks and SPs per year and this at a time when, according to Guderian, Germany's peak production – and that was reached only at the end of 1943 – was 1,000 vehicles per month.

The Soviets could afford to be confident. According to Vassilevsky:

> *The Soviet armed forces had become considerably stronger organisationally, had enhanced their combat skills…the troops' morale was heightened. By the summer of 1943…along the defence lines of the Kursk salient [there was] a powerful grouping consisting of more than 1,330,000 men with over 20,000 field guns, more than 3,500 tanks and 2,650 aircraft…Behind this stood GHQ Reserve, the Steppe Front, with almost 580,000 men, more than 9,000 guns and 1,639 tanks.*

The Soviets had appreciated that this battle was to be a trial of strength and had taken every precaution to ensure that they would emerge victorious. Stavka knew that the Germans could only achieve a victory if they could penetrate quickly through the defensive positions and reach open country, overrunning the Soviet troops before they could organise other lines of defence. The Red Army had learned well, had prepared thoroughly and was confident that it could meet, contain and destroy the imminent German offensive.

Operation *Citadel*, which Hitler had claimed would sound like a fanfare throughout the world, could begin. The rival armies stood ready for battle and waited only upon the hour and time of the Führer's decision.

The Grossdeutschland units reached their form-up positions by 2 July, studied the ground over which they would have to advance and read reports from the divisions holding the front line, which told of only patrol activity by both sides in no-man's-land. Terrain was an important factor during the battle and could almost have been selected specially as the arena in which the great armoured conflicts of the coming days were to be fought. Taking Kursk as the central point, the town lies in the basins of the Don and Dnieper rivers in an area of low hills and open country, undulating in character. In the southern sector it formed part of the central Soviet highland and, in addition to the two major waterways already named, was criss-crossed by the wide valleys of the Seym, Psol, Tim and Oskol rivers. Much of the area was cut by deep ravines which formed natural barriers to an advance from the south and north. There were numerous farms and villages, agriculture being the principal industry. Much of the area was covered with vast fields of maize or sunflowers. There were certain lightly wooded sectors. All in all it was ideal tank country and the principal fighting was to take place for dominant heights, river crossings and the few main roads along which the Red Army supplies came.

Because it was the division which would bear the main brunt of the forthcoming fighting Grossdeutschland had an important pre-battle task and in collaboration with 11th Panzer Division attacked a commanding height to the north of the German front line.

The attack which opened precisely at 14.50hr did not succeed in taking the greater part of the right hand side of the heights until late evening and this initial thrust proved the fears which many had expressed; the Soviet troops were protected by much stronger defences than had been thought, had been well supported by the Soviet Air Force and were thick on the ground. It was only during that night that the whole feature passed into

German control. The first move had been successful.

The units prepared for the opening of the new battle. In the few short hours of darkness, for first light in the Soviet summer comes as early as 02.00hr, the engineers went out to gap the minefields. These obstacles proved to be so thickly sown that one ten-man team lifted 2,700 mines in five hours. The road forward was clear, the artillery officers had their observation posts established, now the operation could begin.

The grand assault opened at 05.00hr on the fine, warm and sunny morning of 5 July. In the fifty-minute barrage which preceded the infantry assaults to the north and south of the salient, more shells were fired by German artillery than had been expended during the whole of the Polish and French campaigns combined. The artillery had spoken, now it was the turn of the armoured fist to strike.

The Grossdeutschland infantry regiments went over the top unaccompanied by their supporting Panthers for these had run into vast minefields. Clausewitz wrote that no battle plan survives the first encounter and on the narrow, 2km wide sector of the Grossdeutschland Division the wildest confusion reigned. Soviet artillery opened fire upon the immobile tanks and then into battle rolled the divisional engineers. They dismounted and calmly lifted the mines, creating gaps through which the advance could continue. All through that long day the squads worked; accepting casualties from shell fire, from snipers and machine-guns, caught up frequently in the counter-attacks which the Red Guard units flung in against the Fusilier groups, trying to fight their way through the artillery fire to reach the objectives.

The Grenadiers had had better luck and in fast, hard-hitting assaults some had crushed all Soviet resistance capturing Point 237 while other battalions of the regiment crossed the torn up land, the wide and deep anti-tank ditches to gain touch with the point unit. Division then switched the main thrust to the Grenadier flank, but infantry alone could not force a breakthrough and the Panthers had run straight into swampy ground in the bed of a small stream and were stuck fast.

Some divisions had broken into the Soviet positions although mud prevented a complete breakthrough and on some sectors attacks were postponed in the hope of the ground drying out but this delay prevented the panzers from penetrating the second line – a vital task of the utmost urgency.

With Grossdeutschland held fast the main thrust passed to 11th Panzer, leaving the Grenadiers and Fusiliers to fight their way slowly forward. On 6 July 2nd Grenadier Battalion went in to assault the second line of the outer Red defences while along the divisional front engineers continued mine-lifting so that the units could strike for their given objectives.

At first the enemy in front of the Grenadiers did not offer such determined resistance and their advance moved quickly forward but unexpectedly, the leading companies then met the main defences of the Soviet second line. The advance slowed in the heavy fire and the Grenadiers began to fight a soldiers' battle, man against man, in the well-built Soviet trenches, the deep dug-outs and the heavily manned strongpoints. By the end of the second day's fighting the battalions were enmeshed in the Soviet trenches. The Fusiliers after bitter fighting had achieved their objective but the divisional front was a salient pushed into the Soviet lines and the whole night was spent under fire from the Red units which bombarded the advanced companies and flung in infantry counter-attacks.

Along the Corps front progress during 7 July had been marked by tank battles and the Soviet armour was more aggressive than formerly. The reason was not hard to find; the Germans had lost air superiority in the southern sector of the salient. As a result of Model's even slower advance, half the air fleet supporting Army Group South had been switched to support 9th Army and the Soviet tanks could concentrate and advance without fear. Nevertheless, by the third day of battle, Corps had reached open country behind the Red defensive positions and was only 11 miles from Oboyan. Thus, 4th Panzer Army had covered half the distance to Kursk and in those 3 fierce days the Soviets had lost 24,000 men as prisoners of war, together with 1,800 tanks and 1,080 anti-tank guns destroyed.

Throughout the rain-sodden 8 July in one attack after another, Soviet armour was sent in against the Grossdeutschland lines. The Soviet losses were enormous and as each assault roared forward, vehicles were picked off by the waiting panzers and the SP guns. The whole divisional front was a graveyard of tanks; shot to pieces, wrecked or burning and yet despite this prodigal expenditure the Soviets had not halted the forward movement of the Grossdeutschland Regiments. But the Germans could not rejoice; their operational timetable was running late and Soviet thrusts and counter-attacks were striking at 4th Panzer Army's flanks and rear.

The Grossdeutschland's assaults went in with and without panzers, with and without the support of the few remaining squadrons of Stukas as slowly the southern pincer clawed its way towards Kursk. The descending spearpoint of 9th Army was making even slower progress. The patterns of the fighting during 9 July remained the same. Slow paced infantry attacks beating off sustained and heavy assaults by Red armour and infantry which poured forward in every type of tactical pattern. Thanks to the close collaboration which still existed with the *Luftwaffe*, the few remaining Stukas bombed the fresh reserves of T.34s waiting to be put into counter-attacks and under the screaming dives of the Ju87s these groups were scattered and could only come to battle in small numbers. Then, suddenly, during the morning it seemed as if the hard and bitter fighting of the past days had broken the Soviet resistance for the remnants of the panzer regiment were able to move quickly across country towards another hill. But this sudden fast move was no breakthrough, for ahead of the panzer were regiments of Soviet tanks and during that day and the one following it the greatest tank battle in the history of warfare was to be fought by 4th Panzer Army and the Red Army.

Let us here reassess the events of the last few days. Stavka realising now that the Southern Front was the most important moved to reinforce it. Vatutin was given two tank Corps from the reserve Army and he had already moved his 1st Tank Army forward and had reinforced it. Stavka then moved 5th Guards Infantry and 5th Guards Tank Armies to support the counter-thrust which General Nikolai Vatutin now felt it was opportune to launch. It was against this fresh Soviet grouping that the exhausted troops of 48th Panzer Corps were now to battle.

The contest which began on 11 July was truly the battle of the Titans. Blocks of armour advanced; waves of tanks poured across the open country; on the ground batteries of artillery fired into the smoke-obscured battlefield; while overhead Stukas dived vertically, like eagles, to bomb the Soviets. By a singular coincidence 48th Corps' thrust, a vast panzer wedge, was rushing towards Soviet tank armies which were themselves coming in at the charge. Two armadas of armour, unknowingly, were about to collide.

From the heights of Point 240 the men of Grossdeutschland could see before them a panorama of combat. Seen dimly through the rain, in and out of the smoke of battle armour, roared in desperate cavalry-type charges; while in an ambush position a squadron could be detected picking off enemy machines. For as far as they could see, and from their front away to their right and out of sight on the sectors held by II SS Corps and 3rd Panzer Corps, the ground was covered with smashed and burning vehicles. From newly hit tanks the crews, dwarfed by the immensity of the machines, could be seen jinking furiously as they made their escape. Dimly seen through the fountains of earth flung up by the shell barrages the observers could see the thin lines of German infantry, moving slowly forward, or else the successive and unbroken infantry waves of a Soviet counter-attack. Here and there a ripple of flame would betray the presence of a Pak front as the anti-tank guns opened fire upon some new panzer thrust.

General Kirill Moskalenko wrote that the tank battles, which were in full swing,

were fought in two areas, south-west of Prokhovovka and in the area of Rzhava…It was hard to tell who was attacking and who was defending…there was no place for manoeuvre. The tankmen were forced to fire point-blank. Villages and heights changed hands repeatedly. The enemy lost heavily…[and] *the Germans were compelled to go over to the defensive…the Nazis had dreamed of reaching Kursk in four days but, in the first eleven days of fighting failed to penetrate deep even into half our defensive lines…*

While, thus, to their flank the mightiest tank battle in history was being fought out – it was to be the swansong of the German panzer force – Grossdeutschland Division continued to move slowly forward until the Oboyan road had been reached. There a halt was made to rest the exhausted infantry. Grossdeutschland consolidated for the night, conscious of the fact that although it had made the deepest penetrations of the entire corps, these had only been achieved at an unbearable rate of loss to both men and machines. Strung out along the line Verchopenye/Oboyan the units waited for the dawn of a new day of battle.

This opened with a pre-emptive thrust by Soviet armour and soon a furious armoured battle was in full swing. With the defeat and withdrawal of the first Soviet tank attack the German panzer went over to the assault. The infantry regiments, too exhausted to continue the forward movement, went temporarily on to the defensive, sending out patrols to gain touch with the units on their flanks.

The strength of the Soviet defence was now so great that along almost the whole divisional front advances were being measured only in metres. Even Strachwitz had been almost halted. The exhausted and fought-out division could advance no further and was able only to hold that ground which it had gained despite the strong Soviet thrusts.

The objective for 12 July was the Psel river and the assault which was to reach that sector was to be made by the Fusiliers supported by armour. Once again the Soviets pre-empted the German thrust and the whole division was forced on to the defensive. Red attacks came in the same traditional formations and at precisely regulated times but the attrition worked and there was hand to hand fighting in the Grossdeutschland infantry positions before the Soviet troops could be expelled.

The Soviet counter-offensive was now in full swing and the division fought back against the Soviet soldiers and tanks which threatened to engulf it.

None of the twenty-two major units on 9th Army's 50km wide sector had made much headway. Model, who had committed his armour in small amounts, had gained less ground than the southern pincer, and his Army had lost great numbers of the 900 tanks with which it had opened the offensive. Stavka, timing its counter-blow on that sector waited until Model was deeply committed and had then opened an offensive against 2nd Army at Orel. This weak and purely infantry force had its front penetrated at a number of points. To guard his back Model had no choice but to withdraw troops fighting in the Kursk salient and to send them to the threatened sectors. The southward drive by 9th Army stagnated and began to fade.

Despite assurances from Manstein that victory was still possible and that the offensive should be allowed to continue, Hitler decided to cut his losses and, rationalising his decision on the grounds that the western Allies had landed in Sicily, cancelled Operation Citadel and redeployed his forces. In this reshuffle the Panzer Grenadier Division Grossdeutschland, together with a panzer division, was posted to Army Group Centre and left the line in the Kursk salient on 18 July. The division's participation in Citadel was at an end.

The failure of this operation left the German Army incapable of holding the front and the Red Army then opened its main summer offensive. Kharkov was recaptured by the Red Army on 23 August and with further great losses of territory the task of the German Army on the Eastern Front was more and more to shield the fatherland and not, as formerly, to be a sword to cut out great expanses of land.

The Germans lost at Kursk and the humiliation was that they had been outfought on a field, and at a time, of their own choosing. But the bitterness of that defeat can be tempered by the fact that at Kursk there occurred a rare happening in the history of warfare where the defending armies were superior to those of the attacker in manpower and weapons.

The Battle to hold the Dnieper Line July-December 1943

The Soviet High Command had planned to begin its 1943 offensive with simultaneous attacks against the Orel and Kharkov salients and such was Stavka's confidence following the fighting at Kursk that almost without a halt, they opened a summer assault which was to last for the next five months and which was to bring their armies, at some points, back to the 1940 frontiers.

The initial Soviet moves brought their forces storming south-westwards on a 30km front, to cut the Briansk/Orel railway line and Grossdeutschland Division was ordered to halt the Soviet drive upon Briansk. The first contacts on 24 July showed that the forces facing the division were Guard infantry. The Soviet drive halted in the face of the Grossdeutschland resistance but then, with a massive build-up their infantry and armour struck forward again during the last week of July and in the initial assault smashed 2nd Panzer Army and captured Orel.

A new offensive on the Byelgorod sector penetrated the German front and forced Army Group South into full and headlong flight. Byelgorod fell and broke the German hold on the northern face of the Kharkov salient. The Ukrainian capital fell on 23rd of the month. Other Red armies then moved forward until seven of them were striking at the weak German line. Along the line of the Mius river 6th German Army was smashed, the Donetz river was crossed and Sokolovsky's armies moved forward upon Smolensk.

The task of Grossdeutschland Division during this period when Army Group South collapsed was to form a shield to protect the Army Group rear while a new defence line was formed behind it. This was no easy task, for the whole of the southern wing was in disarray and Red spearheads were thrusting through almost at will. Faced with the USSR's growing might OKW should have maintained a strong, mobile reserve, but this force had been almost totally destroyed in the great tank battles during Operation *Citadel*.

An optimistic attempt by Army Group to launch Grossdeutschland and some other divisions in an offensive to strike south-eastwards into the Soviet flank at Koeilva opened on 18 August but proved abortive. The Soviet counter-thrust forced Hitler to authorise the evacuation of the Donetz region, to bring the German Army behind the Dnieper river. There had been talk of an 'eastern wall' which had been built to hold back the Soviets along the river line but this was a propaganda myth.

The task of crossing the river was difficult to organise for in Army Group South's sector there were only six bridges and across those structures the whole Army Group would have to pass, including the 200,000 wounded who needed evacuation.

Throughout the long and difficult days and weeks of the withdrawal Grossdeutschland held the rearguard suffering losses which reduced its regiments so that they were amalgamated in order to form battalions. Division was given the task of defending the principal crossing point of the Kremenchug bridgehead and of preventing a Soviet crossing of the river. The first clash between the Grossdeutschland Grenadiers and the Soviet spearheads came during September and on 26th of that month three of Koniev's divisions opened the thrust for Kremenchug. To facilitate the Soviet drive Soviet airborne forces were used and there was savage and bitter fighting as the Grenadiers, supported by Tigers, battled to gain time for Manstein to bring his Army Group back across the river. Under pressure Grossdeutschland was forced back into the eastern outskirts of the city; then into the city where street fighting broke out, Then, having carried out its duty Grossdeutschland began to cross the river on 28 September.

For the next three months Army Group South held Koniev along the line of the Dnieper while in the deep south of the battle line the armies of 2nd Ukrainian Front strove to pin against the sea the German armies which still held out in the Crimea.

The Germans held the Dnieper but had to fight down the Soviet bridgeheads which had been established. As early as 29 September Malinovsky and Vatutin had established lodgement areas. Such had been the impetuosity of the Soviet stormtroops that many had stripped themselves naked and swum across. Others, unwilling to wait for the bridging teams or for a storm boat service to be put into operation, had crossed on planks, empty petrol tins or inflated hides. Whatever means they had used was immaterial; the truth was that the Red Army had bridgeheads crammed full with troops which one day would burst out of the confines and resume the western advance.

In an attempt to drive in one perimeter at Dnieperpetrovsk the Grossdeutschland Division was sent in. In the bitter fighting which marked the next few days German losses were so great that battalions had only company strength and at one time the panzer regiment was reduced to a single vehicle. Only the independent Tiger battalion still had ten machines ready for battle.

To bring the rifle companies up to strength the Grossdeutschland train was drawn on and the men obtained from the non-combatant units were formed into infantry. Only by such methods could the line be maintained and held.

On 15 October the Soviets exploded out of the bridgehead at Mishurin Rog striking to cut communications in the great bend of the Dnieper. The force of this Soviet blow smashed the division's front wide open until the regiments recovered from the shock of the first assault and slowly formed themselves into a rearguard to hold back six Red Armies which were now thrusting for Krivoi Rog. The division's left flank was uncovered; the panzer division which should have held the post had been smashed, but the threatened outflanking was averted by a reconnaissance battalion, one of whose squadrons numbered only nine men. The line held and the Soviets could not take Krivoi Rog at that time but then, on 21 October the Red armour came in against the German forces which had obstructed the advance for a whole week. The Soviets regrouped their forces and flung them forward again on 30 October and smashed 9th Panzer Division, the Grossdeutschland left flank neighbour. Masses of Red armour poured past on the left flank; the right wing then collapsed and more and still more Red tanks swung past Grossdeutschland, still standing grimly blocking the advance upon Krivoi Rog. Then came what was intended by the Soviets to be the coup de grâce. During the misty and rainy morning of 15 November columns of armour and waves of infantry struck the divisional front and by persistent attacks forced the Grenadiers back. During this battle the Soviet armour showed a new tactic that was to be repeated until the end of the war: it no longer bothered to deploy but, as a general rule, accepted losses in an effort to gain ground. But however great were the losses which the Soviet forces suffered, those to Grossdeutschland were even more severe. On one sector, nearly 2km in width, there were only twenty-seven men holding the line. At the end of one severe and costly Soviet assault the 1st Grenadier Battalion numbered an officer and thirteen men. The division was dying and then, when the Red Army was tearing the Germans to pieces, OKW announced that the Western Front was to receive every priority.

The heavy snow of 5 December, the over-extended Soviet supply lines and Grossdeutschland's tenacious defence all combined to halt the Soviet drive until Christmas Day, but then fighting flared again and lasted until the New Year. On that day Soviet infantry stormed forward, shoulder to shoulder, in a succession of attacks, looming out of the thick fog which covered the battlefield and maintaining their assaults from 06.00hr until after dark. The same tactics were repeated on 2 January and then again on 3rd, but by this time Grossdeutschland had been bled almost to death and, unable to obstruct the Soviet drive, had begun to withdraw upon Dynimo.

The divisional remnants were then rushed to Kirovgrad where 2nd Ukrainian Front had broken through and threatened with encirclement the main of 8th Army. As each fresh Soviet thrust broke through the thin crust of the German defence the

Grossdeutschland was moved from one crisis point to another. From Kirovgrad to the valley of the Ssugkleya and from there to the high ground between Fedorovica and Anninska. Each of these fresh assignments had seemingly little point and each of them resulted only in heavy and bitter loss to the division. The given objectives could seldom be gained for the Red Command switched its forces to meet the Grossdeutschland thrusts and beat these into the ground. The division had, however, carried out the task which had been allotted it and had broken the force of Koniev's offensive.

Koniev's armies then went over to an aggressive defence but Stavka could be satisfied with the results which had been achieved in the five-month battle, for now the German line only touched the Dnieper at a small number of places. The Soviets had driven back the German Army from a line behind which it had hoped to gather strength. The 'eastern wall' had proved to be a myth and between Army Group South and Army Group Centre there was a gap of some 100km. Certainly the Soviet strategy of methodical and successive blows along the entire battle front had paid dividends. Now the build-up could begin to open the last series of offensives which would smash the German enemy in the east.

Romania and the defensive battles at Targul Frumos, March-June 1944

The quiet lasted until the first week of March but even in this period of military inactivity patrols were still sent out and losses were still suffered which required the reorganisation of the two infantry regiments and the conscription of the men of the heavy weapons company to form a rifle company.

Hitler had anticipated that mud would halt the Soviet advance but not only had the autumn been dry, but the winter had been mild and the spring rains so light that they had not obstructed the Red Army to any marked degree. Thus the Soviet offensive was reopened just before dawn on 8 March with a box barrage inside which the Red gunners hoped to destroy the Grossdeutschland Division. But defensive plans had been worked out which could now be put into operation. As the blocks of T.34s, JSIIs and the lines of infantry swarmed forward they were brought under German fire and killed in swathes. Even as one rank fell another replaced it until the Soviet lines sweeping forward finally overran some of the Grossdeutschland positions. Hand to hand fighting ensued and small groups of Grenadiers or Fusiliers formed themselves around individual guns, tanks or SPs to fight back the Soviet masses which overwhelmed them. The Red offensive swept away the thin lines of German soldiers holding the front. Those who escaped death or imprisonment as a result of this great holocaust raced back towards the river Bug – the next line of defence.

The Soviet assault was renewed on 9 March and during the hours of darkness the Soviets had built up their forces and at first light sent these forward in great phalanxes of armour. Against this crushing mass the SPs and panzers were switched from one sensitive point of the line to another. Despite the brilliant defensive tactics and the flexibility of Grossdeutschland's units Dynimo fell. In the sweeping advance which followed the Soviets captured Uman on 10 March and the general line of advance for the Soviet forces was now towards the Bug and the Pruth rivers. There could be no defence behind those watercourses; at best they would be only temporary obstacles to the Soviet drive.

The Division once again formed the rearguard while the main of Army Group moved back towards the old frontier. Then came the order for Grossdeutschland itself to move back and the Soviet spearheads marched parallel to those roads along which moved the division's columns. What was to the men of Grossdeutschland a line of withdrawal into safety was for their Soviet enemies the line of advance into German held territory. The race was on; which of the opposing forces would arrive first at the river Bug?

The long columns of German vehicles slithered their way forward while above them aeroplanes of the Soviet Air Force dive-bombed, slowing still further the pace of the retreat, sometimes halting it altogether. En route to Kishinev, the new concentration point, Soviet pressure slackened and the division disengaged itself from the Red forces and was relieved from the line on 14 March.

The aim of Grossdeutschland when it re-entered the combat zone was to bring order out of the chaos which a breakthrough of Soviet armour had wrought. Its main task was to gain time for the German units withdrawing upon Kishinev and the Grenadiers formed a line turned at bay and beat off first one and then a second major assault upon them. To begin with the Grenadiers were alone but then reinforcements came into the area and the line was strengthened with the addition of other infantry battalions and elements from the panzer battalion. Slowly a front was being established, thickened and held.

With the Soviets now across the border into Romania the most important of the tasks facing Stavka was to cut the main highway along which the German troops were supplied. To prevent this the Grenadier rearguard fought back the attacking Red forces and even, where the opportunity allowed it, going over to local counter-attacks. One determined Soviet thrust at Parliti Sat was flung back with such élan that the attacks faded away and for several days there was relative peace in that sector.

Although they were held on one front the Soviets, determined to maintain their progress, struck forward on another sector, infiltrating past Grossdeutschland as the Red Army resumed its march on Jassy. But in their forward movement the Reds presented the flank of their advance to the Grossdeutschland. This was too good an opportunity for the Division to miss. As the Red armour poured past them the Fusiliers flung in a strong attack which not only gained ground but rolling up the Soviet line kept up the advance until it met more determined resistance outside Targul Frumos then smashing aside this more resolute defence the Grenadiers and Fusiliers poured through the town and, scaling the heights, took up position on the high ground to the north and the north-west of the town.

More and more Soviet troops were brought into the area to beat down these German units and the Red forces eventually burst out of their front line zone and resumed their southwards march. Their advance did not go uncontested and sixteen of their T.34s lay smashed and broken on the battlefield. The power of the Soviet thrust was too great and Grossdeutschland fell back to regroup around Bala, where on the 16th, the fighting rose to such a pitch that it was obvious that the main Soviet thrust would come in there.

A panzer thrust against the Soviet forces gathered in the densely wooded area crushed the Red front; the panzer and SPs driving before them the scattered Soviet infantry on to the Grenadiers' machine-guns, while they themselves shot up the immobile blocks of armoured fighting vehicles, which had been drawn up as if for a parade, ready to resume the advance. This successful strike prompted a second assault which went in and further disrupted Soviet preparations for the new offensive. With the enemy dominated, the Grossdeutschland men concentrated on completing work begun to meet the Red assault – digging trenches and laying minefields.

On 26 April the second phase of the Soviet offensive opened with the intent of breaking the German front. At Targul Frumos the Soviet High Command put in more than 400 tanks against Grossdeutschland determined to penetrate the Sereth river valley and in the fierce fighting, 150 Soviet tanks were destroyed. For four days the battle raged and then on Sunday 30 April the Tigers spearheaded a counter-attack led in person by the divisional commander. Inspired by this leadership from the front the Tiger and Panther thrust was irresistible. The Soviet thrust upon Targul Frumos was halted and 56 more of their tanks destroyed.

It had been thought that May Day, the traditional workers' day of celebration, would see the opening of a new assault by the Soviet forces. But the offensive reopened on 2 May heralding three shattering and unceasing days and nights of combat. Behind a sixty-minute drum fire at dawn, two Soviet armies moved into an attack. For as far as the view allowed wedges of Red tanks, and assault infantry detachments, covered the ground and behind these more solid blocks of brown uniformed riflemen waited.

The testing time had come again. The air vibrated to the scream of Katyushas, the ground rumbled with the clattering thunder of tank tracks as the waves of armour rolled over the trenches. Darting in and out among the tank wedges small groups of anti-tank hunters stalked the machines and flung their satchel charges at the tracks. Out of the trenches which the tanks had overrun the Grenadiers and Fusiliers rose up and opened fire upon the Red infantry, holding these off and separating them from the armour and leaving this defenceless against the close quarter attack. Concealed and carefully camouflaged on a flank was a line of 88mm guns and in front of the waiting muzzles passed wedges of JSII tanks with their 120mm main armament. The German guns fired and smashed twenty-five Soviet machines within minutes. Then the Tigers rolled forward and another ten tanks were soon burning. The SPs and panzer combined in one unit and moved forward blowing away with the fury of their guns whole sections of the Soviet line and scything down the Red infantry with the onboard machine-guns.

With the first attack defeated the Soviet main effort then swung to another flank but Grossdeutschland beat that into the ground. A sudden thrust from the west was intercepted and flung back. By midday no less than 250 Soviet tanks had been destroyed. Still, with stubborn but inflexible determination the Soviet commanders hurled their men and machines against the Grossdeutschland. The panzer regiment smashed a further 30 machines in quick succession. As a result of days of such punishment the Soviet thrusts began to lose their ferocity and by the end of the first week of May the front on that sector was quiet.

Division ordered a counter-attack for 7 May to capture a vital hill and the thrust was to be supported by Panther tanks. It is hardly possible to describe the progress of a day in the life of one of the infantrymen in the line fighting in just such an attack: the sudden crushing bombardments; the noisy rocket projectiles; the silent and unheard mortar bomb – a good team could get fifteen in the air in a minute – the naked feeling as flowers and

JSII tanks destroyed during the fighting at Targul Frumos, 1944.

bushes were torn by machine-gun fire only inches above one's head by great bouts of bullets as machine-guns traversed the front. To advance into machine-gun fire and through the great black fountains of earth and smoke of exploding shells, panting with exertion, gasping for breath as the hill became steeper, the grass more slippery, the cover in which to hide more and more sparse. And then, with a heave, to cross the crest and to find trenches full of the enemy and the air thick with hand grenades, machine-pistol fire, shouting and screaming men, frightened, wounded and dying. Then, if the enemy was too strong a rush downhill, crouching to avoid the flying bullets, to halt, reassemble and start the attack again. If the enemy cracked then to keep firing, trembling with drained-off emotion, physical and mental exhaustion. But that was not the end. There were patrols to be sent out, sentries to stand guard and in the dark of the night the sudden rush of an enemy group out to capture a prisoner. Flares, fire and nearly always lukewarm food and never enough water to shake the terrible thirst which combat produced.

That was the pattern for days which the Fusiliers spent in the battle for Point 256. This final spurt by the Grossdeutschland Fusiliers marked the end of Soviet attacks and the beginning of a short period of quiet along the battle line. During this period there was a welcome addition to divisional strength with the arrival of 1029 (Motorised) Grenadier Regiment and, indeed, throughout the whole division changes of the most radical nature were taking place. The strength of the divisional infantry regiments was reduced to three battalions each of four companies and there was an increase in the establishment of armoured and tracked vehicles for the reconnaissance battalion. The division had been nick-named the Führer's Fire Brigade and if it were to fulfil that role then it must be given the most modern vehicles, the fastest firing guns, the highest establishment of the best possible men and materials. And it was.

With renewed signs that the Soviets were planning an advance upon Jassy Grossdeutschland was ordered to strike and to gain high ground on either side of the small town of Orsoaeia. The Red outpost line was quickly pushed in but then the fighting became more intense and many of those who fell were killed in hand to hand combat during the miniature battles which raged in the Carpathian foothills. The spirit of the Grossdeutschland men was irresistible and even the intervention on a massive scale of the Soviet Air Force could not halt the forward movement. On 3 June, Orsoaeia was taken and the bitter fighting again died away for a short time.

The division was withdrawn from the line on 13 June but soon they were to answer the alarm call and be taken across the width of the battle front to East Prussia. Their war in Romania was over but they had held the Soviet thrust for the oilfields of Ploesti and on the battlefields at Targul Frumos and near Jassy they had left their mark. In the more recent fighting, in one five-day period of battle, they had destroyed seventy Soviet tanks, shot down nineteen aircraft, captured forty-five guns and smashed thirty-six anti-tank guns.

The fighting in East Prussia and Latvia, July-October 1944

The rested and refreshed division remained in Romania until the end of July and although the weeks out of the line had enabled the Grossdeutschland to refit and to receive replacements the flow was insufficient to fill out the companies to their full establishment. Recruits were being accepted at seventeen and were being sent up the line after only the most basic training. Nevertheless, the supply of fresh soldiers was drying up and it was with understrength battalions that Grossdeutschland made its way to East Prussia where it encountered yet another grave situation.

The Red Army, revitalised, and with massive reinforcements, was ready to resume its advance. Stavka struck at Army Group Centre aiming to tear a gap in the German battle line which would cause the whole front to collapse.

On 23 June the offensive opened and by 30th the first phase of the battle was over and the destruction of over 20,000 German soldiers had been accomplished. The second phase of the new offensive opened on 4 July 1944 and Minsk fell. In just over a week the new offensive had smashed three German armies and had torn open Army Group Centre which began to collapse. Stavka had now grasped the essentials of flexible command and had conducted the battle with great skill and enterprise. Once one offensive showed signs of weakening then, almost without pause, the flames of a new battle would ignite at some other point. In July 1944 a new offensive opened against the northern part of the German line which smashed the weak front and Red armour spearheads struck towards Baranovichi, Vilna and Dünaberg.

The German Army Groups had little with which they could oppose these virile Soviet thrusts, mounted by a force of some 160 divisions. The drive by 3rd Byelo-Russian Front split Army Group North from Army Group Centre and when Vilna fell on 12 July there rose the very real threat that Army Group North would be cut off. True to his usual practice Hitler refused to countenance any withdrawal. While Army Group was being constricted more closely in the Vilna area, pressure lessened on other sectors allowing 4th Army and 3rd Panzer Army to form a cohesive though weak front along the line of the Niemen river.

The Soviets then swarmed forward once again but were held in those sectors of 3rd and 4th Armies. Rather than waste time and manpower in battling their way through, the Soviet Command again swung the main effort of its offensive against Army Group North. To cut that Group completely off some Red Army units were sent on outflanking drives and by 21 July had reached Ponevich some 150km west of Dunaberg. From that town they regrouped and struck forward towards Riga. With the fall of the capital of Latvia, Army Group North was completely isolated and on the German left flank there yawned a wide gap through which Soviet armour poured westwards. The only German troops which were available to be committed to action was a group of units which had originally been brought together to mount an offensive to link the northern and central Army Groups. There could now, in the face of this new thrust, be no point in seeking to link the separated Army Groups; now every available unit must be flung in to hold the crumbling line.

The main of Grossdeutschland neared the end of its concentration on 3 August and, as each fresh divisional unit arrived, it was sent out on reconnaissance to establish the whereabouts of the Soviet spearheads and to gain touch with the formations on either flank. This latter task produced a wave of alarm in the Grossdeutschland units for many of the flank contingents were locally-raised detachments of Landsturm men, long past military age, or young and under-age boys. The formations upon which the defence of the Reich now depended were untrained recruits in an unfortified position backed by burnt-out Army divisions.

During the first week of August the Soviet offensive along the Vistula began to slow down and Stavka struck new blows on other sectors.

On that held by Grossdeutschland the first divisional unit into action was the Tiger battalion which was put in near Vilkovishken to stem the Soviet flood. Despite the most strenuous efforts of the crews, the Tigers could not stop the Soviet forces from threatening the highway which ran from Gumbinnen to Vilkovishken. As soon as other divisional units arrived in the concentration area south of Wirballen they were ordered to attack to gain touch with left flank units. A Grossdeutschland battle group went out and gained ground until the main Soviet defence zone was approached and to revive the faltering advance a Tiger company was sent in but lost four machines in the fierce fighting. The German advance was halted on that sector and the Grossdeutschland units were drawn out from the line and sent in during the foggy morning of 9 August to capture Vilkovishken in a swift and silent assault. There was no heralding barrage as the panzer and Grenadiers roared across the flat and open fields, shrouded in mist which hid them from the observant eyes of the Soviet artillery observers. But then as the morning advanced and the sun rose higher dispersing the fog the attacking formation was exposed to view and a thunder of shell fire was poured down upon it. With the first group battling its way through concentrated fire, a second column drove off towards the town despite the assaults of fighter bombers, heavy artillery and Katyusha rockets. The swing of the attack brought it forward before minefields and swampy ground halted the forward movement. Ground conditions had halted the armour but the Grenadiers were not to be gainsaid and they stormed forward on foot broke through and smashed the crack regiments of a Red Guard Corps.

Working with their usual industry the Soviet troops had had time to turn Vilkovishken into a little fortress and house to house battles marked 9 August as the Grossdeutschland Grenadiers fought their way forward through the little market town. From house to house, from garden to garden the Grenadiers battled with the Red Guards, stalking the Red armour with *Panzerfaust* and with their fast firing MG 42s crushing the infantry assaults as they poured out of the maize fields. Not until last light was the town captured and consolidated, though all through the night patrols were active destroying the last small pockets of Soviet resistance.

The ORW counter-measures on the central front had stemmed the great Soviet offensive which had covered the 600km from the upper Dnieper to the Vistula in six weeks and as new offensives opened on the northern sector Grossdeueschland was ordered to break through to the encircled Army Group North. The first objective, Kursenai, was too strongly held and the assaulting forces too weak for them to capture it, but the Grenadiers then launched a swift, silent and successful night attack. The advance continually gained ground, but formed also a salient which could not be held. A slow, reluctant withdrawal began and on 22 August the division was put in to strengthen an attempt, on a fresh sector, to break through to Army Group North. A group of panzer divisions had already opened the assault and by their efforts had brought point units to within 35km of the Army Group's outpost line. The assault began to fade and Grossdeutschland went in to revive it. Strachwitz's panzer detachment broke through to Tukkum and began to push on towards Riga, followed by the other panzer divisions which expanded the gap which had been created.

The Grossdeutschland assault began to lose impetus in the minefields and swamps and Stavka reinforced the Red Army units on that sector and flung in counter-attacks backed by massed artillery. Soon the Grossdeutschland was losing men at an alarming rate and in most battalions the only officer still left was the commander, while whole platoons were being led by corporals or even grenadiers. With companies now reduced to less than forty men the advance died away for lack of manpower to sustain it. The intention to relieve Army Group North had to be abandoned and the Grossdeutschland, although still kept in the line, went over to a defensive posture.

On 4 October the signs that a revived Soviet offensive in East Prussia was imminent forced OKW to withdraw the division from the line and to regroup it as the Army's counter-attack reserve.

The new Red Army offensive was launched by a great force of nineteen infantry divisions, three tank corps and an artillery corps massed upon a narrow front. The Soviets poured across the Venta river destroying the German bridgehead there and swept aside, almost without halting to meet them, the counter-attacks which Grossdeutschland launched against it. The town of Luoke was considered to be vital to the German defence and during 7 October Grossdeutschland was ordered to hold it at all costs and thereby to halt the Soviet drive. The Soviet tactic of mass armoured columns not bothering to deploy allowed Grossdeutschland anti-tank gunners, SPs and the remaining armoured fighting vehicles to gain many 'kills', but the Red armada was constantly replenished from the vast reserves which Stavka had gathered during the months of seeming inactivity.

The Soviet advance poured past Luoke and the Grosdeutschland garrison. There followed a withdrawal to Gaduvannas but the Soviet command was not interested in petty obstructions to its advance and swung the main advance towards Memel. Once again Grossdeutschland was forced to react to a Soviet move and the division was ordered to reach and to support the defence inside this strategically important town. To achieve this order the Grossdeutschland battalions fought their way through the Soviet forces which were infesting the city.

Six

Panzer Corps Grossdeutschland in the Battle for Germany, 1944-45

As early as 7 August OKW knew that the moves it had made and the troops which it had put into action had halted the great offensive. German resistance was, however, not the chief reason the Soviet movement ended, rather it was logistics which had, once again, acted as a brake on Stavka plans.

From its start line the grand assault had covered a distance of nearly 750km and had accomplished this in only six weeks fighting during which Army Group Centre had collapsed. At the beginning of August the offensive halted and there was to be a lull while the Soviet forces south of the river Bug were regrouped, reinforced and resupplied.

The previous chapter indicated how OKW had been forced to deploy to the centre troops from other sectors of the Eastern Front, leaving those dangerously weakened and a temptation to the planners at Stavka. The German Supreme Command knew that the Red Army could mount an attack wherever and whenever it chose, selecting that point at which its attacks would gain the greatest benefit. This and the knowledge of its own Army's impotence alarmed the officers at OKW.

The nearness of the Soviet Army to Germany herself brought home to the Reich Government how vulnerable she was and certain defensive measures were taken. These were too little and too late to avert the final catastrophe, but they were able, to some degree, to slow down the pace of the final Soviet onslaught when it came in 1945. Among those measures was the announcement that the eastern provinces of Germany had become the Eastern Fortified Area and that an 'eastern wall' was to be constructed. The grandiose titles had little significance except that of a propaganda value. Rather more unfortunate, for the civilian population, was that the *Gauleiter* had greater powers than the local military commanders in respect of the conscription of labour to build defences and the formation of the *Volkssturm*.

The chief causes of friction between the military and the Party were on the questions of when to order evacuation of civilians from likely battle zones and when to muster the *Volkssturm*. The Army had begun the evacuation of Memel as early as August for it was aware that East Prussia was soon to become a battle area. Stavka decided to open its new offensive in that province.

It was at this time that new ideas on the establishment and use of major units were undertaken. To understand the significance of these new ideas we must return to summer 1943 when Operation *Citadel* failed. From that time on the German Army on the Eastern Front was to gain no more offensive and strategic victories. It did achieve strategic victories but these were defensive ones and it did carry out offensives, but these were local and tactical. From the end of summer 1943 the military defeat of Germany was assured; the end was merely a question of time.

The losses in men and in material during that year had already been catastrophic. The defeat of 6th Army at Stalingrad had been followed by the surrender of Panzer Army Africa and following close upon those two disasters had come the failure of Operation *Citadel* with its fearful casualties in men and machines. The serious shortage of infantry meant an inadequately manned forward defence zone. There were vast areas left undefended and there was nothing to hold back the enemy save mobile patrols whose operational range was limited by the critical shortage of fuel.

It was then that new concepts of defence were designed, fresh ideas introduced to reshuffle the available forces and new weapons brought into service to compensate for the infantrymen who were lacking.

The SS organisation facing the same manpower crisis as the Army, had seized upon the obvious solution and had combined units to form permanent corps. The Army, not wishing to be laggard in its own organisation, saw the advantages to be gained from the SS scheme and took it a stage further by proposing, during the discussions which went on during the autumn of 1944 that these permanent Corps be all-armoured. It was proposed that the Grossdeutschland and the Brandenburg Divisions be amalgamated to form one Corps and that a Führer Corps made up of the Begleit, the Grenadier Brigades and the Wach Regiment also be raised. The latter Corps were never formed.

It is understandable that Grossdeutschland should have been selected since for most of its active service life it had served as the Führer's Fire Brigade. Its successes in this role had convinced OKW that Germany's last military hope rested on elite units which were equipped with the best vehicles, the pick of the recruits and a higher than normal establishment of the most modern weapons to enable them to carry out their specialist duties.

To ensure that the future Panzer Corps Grossdeutschland obtained the units it needed detachments were taken from a number of sources to form Corps troops. The remnants of 12th Corps and the command units of 18th Artillery Division were seconded to Grossdeutschland headquarters where the proposed amalgamation of the two divisions was to take place. The infantry strength of the new Panzer Corps was to be increased by another regiment; there was to be a heavy tank battalion and an armoured artillery regiment.

The tragedy was that the amalgamation came too late in the war and that when it was once established both constituent divisions were separated and posted to different sectors of the front and thus did not fight as a single unit.

It is even more ironic when it is realised that temporarily forming a corps with the Grossdeutschland Division in Prussia was 1st Division of the Hermann Göring Para/ Panzer Corps while the 2nd Division of that Corps was the partner of Brandenburg in its fight south of Berlin.

The next stage in Stavka's operational plan was to clear the northern flank by destroying the German forces in Latvia and Lithuania and to accompany this by a thrust through East Prussia to the Baltic. This would leave Army Group North's units isolated from each other, cut off from Germany and with their backs to the Baltic sea.

The thrust which 5th Guards Tank Army and 43rd Army then made, sealed the ring around the Memel garrison which included Grossdeutschland Division. Memel had been a supply base for the army fighting in the Soviet Union and the four divisions of its garrison did not suffer the shortages of shells and fuel which had been the lot of the units fighting on the eastern front. There was an abundance of the materials needed to withstand a long siege. The most elaborate fire plans could be worked out and any call for help by an infantry unit under pressure from a Soviet attack could be answered by a rain of shells upon the advancing Red Army. To support the field artillery, warships of the German Navy cruised along the coast bombarding the Soviet positions with their 11in guns.

Despite this material plenitude and the garrison's aggressive defence the situation was an unsatisfactory one, for Memel was completely cut off and was little more than a tactical problem to the Soviet High Command. Neither it, nor indeed, any of the Baltic towns which Hitler had ordered must be held to the last, had any strategic value and only served to bottle up German divisions which could have been used on other sectors and in more mobile roles.

The Soviet assaults with tanks, SPs and infantry masses which came in against Grossdeutschland's front during 14 October were patterns of the other assaults which were to be repeated during the weeks in which the city held out. At the end of that first day of the offensive sixty-six Soviet tanks lay smashed, of which total Grossdeutschland units had destroyed thirty-six. The siege dragged on into November but the Grossdeutschland Division was not to remain imprisoned in Memel. The threat of resumed Soviet attacks in East Prussia required strong forces in that province and the garrison in Memel was drawn upon to supply some of these. Panzer Grenadier Division Grossdeutschland was posted to East Prussia where its amalgamation into a Panzer Corps was to take place.

Starting on 21 November and completed by 4 December the division was taken by sea to Königsberg, leaving the garrison of Memel to fight on. The attack against that city had been the signal for a renewed assault upon East Prussia by three Red Armies. Defending the long battle line from Memel to Novgorod on the Narev was 4th Army with four infantry and one panzer corps. A Soviet penetration was held by the intervention of a flak battalion, parts of a para infantry regiment and *Volkssturm* battalions. The 4th Army then scraped together a counter-attack group, including the Führer Begleit Brigade which established a firm front during the first week of November after which the Soviet assaults died away and had ceased by the middle of the month.

Halted temporarily in the north Stavka then shifted the offensive to Hungary and sent in 2nd and 3rd Ukrainian Fronts against Army Groups A and South. Marshal Rodion Malinovsky's armies advanced rapidly towards the Danube. Although Budapest was to hold out against an investing Soviet force for several months, Hitler came to the astonishing deduction that Germany's fate would not be decided on the main eastern front, along the Vistula, a river outpost protecting Berlin, but in Hungary. Once again he raised the alarm that unless this or that commodity could be obtained or regained by some fresh offensive then the war was lost. On this occasion the vital, war-winning material without which Germany would crash down into ruin, was to be found in Hungary.

From the battle hardened units holding central Poland new sacrifices were demanded. Divisions which were to have formed a bulwark against the Red onslaught were despatched southwards and their place in the line was taken by newly raised formations; units so raw and so recently formed that the component regiments were generally unknown to each other. Grossdeutschland was not involved in these manoeuvres at first being left unmolested to carry out its transformation into a Panzer Corps. But barely had the first elements of Brandenburg Division begun to arrive in the concentration area than Grossdeutschland Panzer Corps HQ was ordered to despatch a division to East Prussia to counter the offensive which had reopened along the line of the Vistula. Panzer Grenadier Division Grossdeutschland, the only one of the two divisions of corps up to strength, was thereupon sent north-eastwards heading for the sound of the guns and ready to form the northern shoulder of the battle line of Army Group Centre.

The sector held by that Army Group was nearly 600km long; only a fraction of those enormous lengths of front which once the German Army Group had manned in earlier years, but now even such short distances were beyond its strength. Three veteran but weakened armies held this front: in the north 3rd Panzer, on its right 4th Army and with 2nd Army holding the southern post. As a consequence of the fighting which had now flared up in Hungary there was a lessening of pressure against Army Group Centre permitting a withdrawal of some divisions from the line for rest and refitting. Drafts of men filled out the depleted regiments, more potent weapons came into service and the whole Army Group, although understrength and outnumbered, was made ready to meet the forthcoming Soviet offensive.

Against those three German Armies the Soviets placed the combined forces of three whole fronts and part of a fourth: Zhukov's 1st Byelo-Russian; 2nd Byelo-Russian Front under Rokossovski; and, in the south, under General Ivan Chernakovski, 3rd Byelo-Russian Front. Koniev's 1st Ukrainian Front, which was to open the new offensive, would strike in its assault Army Group's right wing and also the left wing of Southern Army Group.

Soviet strategy was to separate Army Groups Centre and A and to destroy them in isolation. Koniev would thrust along the Lemberg/Czenstochau line to rupture the front of Army Group A. Almost simultaneously 1st Byelo-Russian Front would strike south of Warsaw and head towards Berlin. To ensure the success of the major assault by its right wing forces the Soviets had gathered a mass whose supremacy was shattering. In infantry there was a majority of 11:1 in the Soviet favour; in tanks the imbalance was 7:1; while in artillery for each single piece that the Germans could put into the line, the Soviets could match it with 20. There were 163 Red infantry divisions and armoured brigades, the whole totalling over two million men with 6,000 tanks and over 30,000 field guns, not including mortars of every type. This host was to be launched in the first great battle of the sixth year of the war. D-Day for the opening of the offensive was 12 January and zero hour was 03.30hr.

The situation facing Germany was a desperate one. Assaulted from the west, threatened from the south and battered in the east the German armies had retreated almost to the former borders of the Reich. And during these months of despair one after the other of their allies had left them: Bulgaria, Romania and Hungary had each sued for peace and had been occupied by the advancing and victorious Red Army. In the months of battle which lay ahead units from Panzer Grenadier Division Grossdeutschland, from Corps headquarters the Brandenburg, the Führer units and Panzer Grenadier Division Kurmark – widely separated from each other but each stiffening the front wherever it stood – battled, bled and died. None of them was to go down in a spectacular, Wagnerian *Götterdämmerung,* rather they were to be scattered and were to be destroyed; little groups of men fighting against superior odds, in battles which were generally unrecorded and unremarked.

Hitler's offensive in December 1944, to capture Antwerp by an attack through the Ardennes had failed completely and the two Führer Brigades had been pulled out and were en route back to the Eastern Front where the new Soviet offensive was about to be unleashed. Aerial reconnaissance and first hand knowledge of the terrain enabled Army Group Centre's planners to forecast with a high expectancy of accuracy the avenues along which the Soviet advance would be made and the few available counter-attack divisions were moved forward to take up positions from which they would strike back at the Soviet sea of armour.

The whole front from the Baltic to Hungary waited for the dawn of 13 January 1945.

The battle for the Vistula, January 1945

The three-hour long barrage which opened during the night of 12 January struck and shattered 4th Panzer Army. In the confusion, dark and chaos of that bitter winter day the shock of the initial blow was heightened by waves of Red Air Force machines which came to strafe anything which had survived the artillery bombardment. Rolling through narrow lanes in the gun line, where the artillery pieces stood almost wheel to wheel in the snow covered fields, the vehicles of two tank Corps roared down upon the German lines. Red Army men rode on the tanks, huddled close behind the vehicles or, if they formed the third wave, trudged forward in column singing as they marched into battle. Fourteen divisions of Red infantry followed the tanks as they poured through the ruptured German front. By the end of that day the gap had been extended to a width of over 35km.

As the flood poured westwards, German divisions cut off from their Corps, regiments isolated from their divisions and battalions out of touch with their regiments fought against impossible odds. Here a unit would be overrun and destroyed immediately; at some other place an artillery regiment with its gunners grim-faced around their weapons, fired upon the approaching waves of Soviet armour and continued to load, aim and fire until it went under – leaving on the blackened snow the empty shell cases, the stiffening dead, the shattered gun barrels and the smashed burning hulks of the tanks which it had destroyed. 250 were smashed on that first day. Towards the gap torn in the German line, tanks of other Soviet armies were directed and by the dawn of 13th Koniev's Ukrainian Front had begun to pass into the breach.

The counter-attacks which OKW then launched were as futile as they were predictable. The 4th Panzer Army had no reserves of its own and the few units which Hitler permitted to move out of the general reserve were too weak and were put in too late to affect the course of the fighting. They were caught up in the maelstrom of battle and their soldiers died frequently unaware of where they were or what was the objective of their mission. Bewildered and outnumbered the fighting life of these sacrificed units was measured in hours at the worst, in days at the best and those who survived the holocaust were scraped together into other ad hoc groupings and then sent back up the line.

Stavka had ordered the 2nd Byelo-Russian Front to attack in succession to the Ukrainian Front and to smash towards Germany proper. Then East Prussia was to be attacked from the east by 3rd Byelo-Russian Front and isolated from the rest of Germany by the north-westerly swing of 2nd Byelo-Russian Front. To the south 1st Byelo-Russian Front was poised to strike for the upper Oder while on its left 1st Ukranian Front would drive for Silesia and for Bresiau.

It was at this time, when the direction of the first Soviet thrust had become apparent, that Hitler ordered Grossdeutschland Panzer Corps HQ and the Brandenburg Division to move down upon Lemberg and, during its drive, to close the gaps which had been made in the line of Army Group South.

During the time that the paths of two constituent divisions of Grossdeutschland Panzer Corps were diverging, never to meet again, the breach in the 4th Panzer Army's sector was widened as the Red Army's virile thrusts trapped 24th Panzer and 42nd Corps in pockets within which it seemed that all hope must have died. The commander of 42nd Corps was, however, an old hand and the survivor of many encirclement battles. He knew that cohesion counted. He joined his force to that of 24th Panzer knowing that as long as the two corps marched as a single pocket then it would always be stronger than any Soviet formations it might encounter. The sick or wounded would be carried on vehicles, unless their wounds were such that the journey might kill them. Then these little bands of badly injured men, tended by volunteer groups of medical officers and orderlies would be left behind, while the pocket rolled on westward. During the night of 17 January, the break out by 42nd Corps was ordered. The heaviest armour formed the point unit with lighter armour on the flanks; SP guns guarded the rear. And 42nd Corps began a period of fighting which was to last until it had linked up with 24th Panzer and which both Corps were then to endure until they had battled through to the outposts of Grossdeutschland Corps HQ on the banks of the Warthe river. Day after day the pattern remained constant. The men holding off furious assaults in day-long battles which were broken off at last light. The outlying picquets would then be called in and then the pocket would resume its march through the bitter cold of an eastern winter night.

Along the embattled front the Red Army's hammer blows struck simultaneously, struck individually and in rotation. They struck in a synchronised tattoo or in a rapid succession of blows and whole German divisions were driven to destruction and annihilation. These died in the silence of the great forests; they died with their men perishing in thousands, frozen on the icy hills or on the open plains which afforded no protection against the knife-edged winds.

Within days of the opening of the great offensive Rokossovski's army was racing to reach the Baltic with the intention of isolating Army Group Centre. Panzer Grenadier Division Grossdeutschland was then ordered to carry out a two-fold task. With one effort it would form a new defence line and while this was being established it would send out battle groups to seal off the gaps in the front line. One of the first units of the Grossdeutschland Division to go into action was the Fusilier Regiment which, on 15 January, supported by a Grenadier battalion of a neighbouring division, pushed south-westwards towards the village of Stegma.

The fighting was typical of a thousand small actions being fought at that time. Across whole sectors of the front there was no continuous line of defence. Villages, hamlets and small towns had been converted into strong points between which ranged German patrols. The front was everywhere. The roar of tank engines at one place would herald the assault by an armoured wave upon the small garrison. Three or four kilometres away only a distant rumble of gunfire would betray that the war was within hearing distance. The Soviet troops seemed just as unfamiliar with the battle pattern. One Fusilier battalion, fighting with a frenzy born of desperation, was suddenly astonished to see approaching its hard defended positions, a battalion of Red Army infantry striding out in column of route and as carefree as if they were on manoeuvres. To the Grossdeutschland Fusiliers this target was a reward for the battering to which they had been subjected and all ranks waited patiently as the brown-uniformed column moved into range. Under the rapid and continuous hail of bullets the front files of the Red battalion melted away and the slowness in deploying meant death for most of the survivors. Soon along the road lay the dead and wounded of a Soviet battalion which had believed itself to be safe within its own lines.

Then into the battle roared the vehicles of a panzer company and with high explosive shells began to blow apart the huddled groups of Soviet infantry seeking shelter from the Fusiliers' machine-guns.

Four years of war had, however, heightened the efficiency of Red Army communications and within the hour an artillery bombardment had begun to fall upon the Fusiliers. Hour after hour the gunfire echoed among the white hills and destroyed the German positions. Behind the shells came the waves of tanks and infantry. Swooping down upon the Grossdeutschland units forced out of their trenches by the fury of the bombardment came the Cossacks sabring the machine-pistolling hard pressed Fusiliers.

The Fusiliers' attack upon Stegma had been stopped dead and flung back. Here and there companies still strove to maintain the advance fighting for hamlets and crossroad villages, trying to wrest these from the determined Soviet defenders. Against these few German attackers, struggling slowly forward through artillery and mortar barrages the Soviet commanders could group masses of men. During one assault an isolated and scattered group of machine-gunners saw before them lines of Red Army infantry extending from left to right as far as the eye could see. Line followed line, moving forward inexorably upon Grossdeutschland which was bleeding to death.

In the middle of this battle Grossdeutschland was suddenly posted to Army Group A, there to seal a break in its front along the Vistula. Under normal conditions relief of a unit in a forward sector is a delicate task. To carry out such an operation when the infantry is locked in battle is an almost impossible task. The Grenadiers were ordered to break off the fighting and to race on foot across the open country, during which they were bombarded by Red Artillery and machine-gunners firing over open sights. The losses were frightful and the scattered survivors, quickly concentrated, were mounted on armoured vehicles ready to move into action under the command of a new Army.

The division was being torn to pieces and as an example of its losses only four guns of the anti-tank battalion survived after that unit had been overrun.

In East Prussia the Panzer Grenadier Division Grossdeutschland was involved in bitter fighting: the Führer Divisions, recently elevated from brigade status, were moving towards Stettin; the Panzer Division Kurmark, raised from the Grossdeutschland replacement depot, was preparing to move to Liegnitz; and the Panzer Grenadier Division Brandenburg, together with Grossdeutschland Corps HQ, was down in the great Vistula bend holding open the crossings across the Warthe river towards which the marching pocket of 24th Panzer and 42nd Corps was moving.

The whole front was ablaze and in movement as the outnumbered and battered German troops were forced back, penetrated, bypassed, encircled and destroyed. Under tremendous pressure 9th Army fell back and evacuated Warsaw which was captured by 1st Polish Army of Zhukov's Command on the 17th. Cracow was taken on 19th and a guards armoured unit crossed the former Polish/German frontier and entered Silesia on the 20th. Other Soviet tank forces pressed the advance forward until on 22 January 1945, a reconnaissance battalion of 5th Guards Army stood on the banks of the Oder river.

Near to that area through which the Red Army had raced stood the Brandenburg Division and Grossdeutschland Corps HQ holding bridgeheads on the Warthe river waiting for the two encircled corps to reach them. The last miles of that retreat for 24th and 42nd Corps were a calvary but finally, after a march of 250km, 16th Panzer Division made contact with the Grossdeutchland outposts. Throughout the next few days the battered but undefeated remnants of both corps passed through the Grossdeutschland bridgehead.

Army Group Centre was disintegrating. A Soviet drive fragmented a German corps on the Narev river and 2nd Army's inevitable rearward movement was exploited by Soviet armour which forced its way through the defensive lines and struck for Elbing. It fell to 7th Panzer Division, Rommel's 'Ghost' Division of the 1940 campaign in France, which carried out what was possibly the last major German tank battle of the Second World War, when it engaged the onrushing Soviet spearheads. By efforts that can scarcely be comprehended the 7th Panzer fought its last great fight and by the end of that dreadful time the 25th Panzer Regiment had died; but in the fields and village streets, smashed and burning lay the hulks of 200 Red Army tanks.

By the 26th the Soviet forces reached the Baltic. A thin armoured wedge of Soviet tanks had cut off from the main German forces both the 4th Army and the 3rd Panzer Army. Army Group Centre was dead. The two cut-off armies, together with certain other units in East Prussia, were retitled Army Group North.

By the 22nd along Warthe river a Red Guards unit had forced the river line at Treskau but had been held there. On other sectors, however, 9th Army was forced back towards the Oder, separating it completely from 2nd Army. Along the roads leading towards Germany there was complete chaos. Military units ordered to withdraw and to form fresh defensive lines in the rear found themselves trapped on roads which were jammed with convoys of refugees all hoping by foot marches to escape the Red armour which was cutting through the fragmenting German front. Each air attack left dead and dying blocking the highways and halting the forward flow of troops to the front and the withdrawal of train units from the battle zone.

Desperately, the troops of 2nd Army tried to stem one major armoured breakthrough east of Praschwitz. High Command sent the Panthers of No. 4 Company of Grossdeutschland's 1st Panzer Battalion to halt this drive. Along icy roads, across frozen fields and taking up ambush positions along the Soviet line of advance the Grossdeutschland Panzer destroyed six vehicles of the Red point unit and flung back the remainder in confusion. While the Soviet forces were thus held on that sector men of the Fusilier Regiment mounted a miscellany of vehicles and dashed to Mielau to defend that threatened town.

Such moves were too late for even as they took up position along the Orzyc river came disturbing news that the Red Army had avoided a direct confrontation and was advancing, albeit slowly, along the division's southern flank. In an attempt to smash into the flank of the Red Army's drive upon Mielau the Grenadier Regiment carried out an unsupported infantry assault, advancing in a blizzard which cut visibility to only yards. Cohesion between the isolated groups of German infantry, struggling forward through the snow, was soon lost and then, during a sudden lull in the snow storm, the lines of the Grenadiers were exposed and visible to the Soviet artillery observers. The storm of shells which struck their thin line crushed it. The attack was halted; the Grenadier wave receded.

The way was now clear for the Soviet troops to advance towards Mielau and under this pressure Grossdeutschland was forced back upon the town. So fast was the pace of the Soviet drive that their forward elements reached Mielau before the town had been put into a proper state of defence and their thrusts had to be fought back by hastily formed battle groups. Motorised and panzer units were now severely restricted by the shortage of fuel for the vehicles. Tanks consumed precious petrol in towing other vehicles or guns into the perimeter which was being formed around East Prussia, and so slow was the movement of these columns that at Neidenburg the Soviets had had time to set up a road block of massed anti-tank guns – a pak front – backed by heavy, armoured units. For Grossdeutschland moving towards it there could be no turning back; behind them were other Red formations; the shortage of petrol precluded any attempt at skirting the barrier. The only solution was to advance and smash through the block. During the ensuing battle all the soft-skinned vehicles were destroyed and the panzer battalions suffered such heavy losses that when the German units regrouped, many tank companies were found to have been reduced to a single vehicle. In the infantry battalions many companies now numbered only thirty men, while the artillery component, which had lost a whole battery overrun at Niedenburg, had had its SP detachments almost completely destroyed.

The weakened division was forced further and further northwards. Even in strong defensive positions the withdrawal of other units, the loss of towns or the momentum of the Soviet pressure demanded the withdrawal of the Grossdeutschland units deeper into East Prussia.

Allenstein fell on 22 January and the Soviet ring around the province was drawn tighter. The division received orders that Königsberg, capital of the province, which had been cut off by the Soviet drive, was to be relieved by an advance from Kreuzberg intended to open the road and to raise the siege.

Back in Berlin the acute danger of a total collapse of the Eastern Front was becoming apparent and the first troops were rushed from the west to the Oder river. To co-ordinate the military activity on that front Army Group Vistula was formed on 21 January.

It was now the end of January. The Soviet offensive was beginning to show signs of running out of momentum. Supply difficulties were denying the Soviet forward units the fuel and ammunition which alone could nourish the advance. The speed of the Red assault in the centre slowed perceptibly but on the northern flank facing East Prussia the Red Armies, with shorter lines of supply, kept up the pressure even though the tough German defence reduced the speed of the advance.

It was into the western flank of those forces investing Königsberg that the Fusiliers and the remaining Tigers were to thrust in the last panzer assault carried out by Grossdeutschland during the war.

The last battles of the Panzer Grenadier Division Grossdeutschland in East Prussia, January-May 1945

It was during these last fearful months that Hitler began to move whole armies about the battle fronts as if they were chess pieces. For weeks on end first-class formations, despatched at the whim of the Supreme Commander, from one front or from one sector to another, were absent from the battle line while their vehicles and men were shunted backwards and forwards across Germany. Their moves not only kept these units out of the fighting but tied up rolling stock, overstraining a railway system suffering from the effects of Allied air bombardment.

In one such panic deployment, troops had been rushed from the Western Front to Army Group Vistula but the pace of the Soviet advance had been faster than that of the German units. By 3 February, and Guards Armoured Army and 5th Assault Army forced bridgeheads across the Oder.

The whole of eastern Germany was embattled. Memel had been evacuated, the armies of Army Group Centre had been torn apart from each other and the best efforts of Army

Group Vistula could not close the gaps which separated them. Königsberg had succeeded Memel as the area which 4th Army had to hold as its northern bastion and the city was the next natural objective in the progress of the Soviet offensive. By 24 January the Soviets had reached Elbing and all 4th Army's efforts to break out westwards were flung back. Deeply aware of his inferiority vis à vis the Red forces, 4th Army Commander ordered his troops to take up a defensive posture.

The Army's defence of Königsberg was based upon the town itself, the thin area of the Haff to the south-west of the town which Grossdeutschland had captured and the bridgehead between Braunsberg and Zinten. During the succeeding weeks the German garrisons in those sectors improved their positions and one successful effort forced a narrow corridor through which the civilians passed down to an evacuation point and were taken off by ship. Not all the attacks had such fortunate outcomes and one carried out by the Fusiliers and Tiger tanks in a snowstorm, was beaten back by a Red pak front. At other places and at other times during the fighting at the turn of the year the Grossdeutschland infantry regiments were involved in house to house fighting for Jäskheim. As they moved out of the houses the Grenadier groups became the target for concentrated artillery barrages and charges by Cossacks which rode out of the blinding blizzards, sabring left and right the Grenadiers as they broke under the fierce and sudden assaults. But the enemy could not halt the Grenadiers' forward movement.

Against other Grossdeutschland positions in the south-western suburbs of Königsberg the Soviet infantry probed, seeking weak spots, testing the alertness of sentries, infiltrating snipers and trying to pass round the divisional front and to isolate the Grossdeutschland groups one from the other. The divisional commander, deeply conscious of how tenuous was the life-line, ordered an attack southwards to widen the corridor and to cut the motorway which nourished the Soviet assault troops. The German attack went in across the flat, open and snow-covered fields of Prussia but was driven back. Again and again the battalion commanders led their men forward but their efforts collapsed in the fury of the Soviet fire. When the battle ended, 3rd Grenadier Battalion had been reduced to only fifty men. During 4 February a second attempt to break out of the city met with greater success. Some groups then passed into reserve while the remainder maintained their attacks with the aim of strengthening the line or of clearing salients.

The division was not now fighting as an homogenous whole and in the closing weeks of February some of its units were further split up and posted to stiffen the line with other divisions.

The fighting had now taken on the dimensions of the battles of the First World War. There were no longer advances of a hundred or more miles, nor even a dozen miles. Ground lost or gained was measured in metres and there was heavy and continual fighting for even individual houses and farm buildings. For the isolated Grenadier groups holding the ruins of some shattered East Prussian home there was little respite from the incessant attacks by waves of infantry and armour. Khaki clad Soviet infantry might gain a foothold in part of a house, and small groups of Grenadiers, the last remnants of the counter-attack force, would be hurried forward to expel the incursors with machine-pistol fire and hand grenades. For days the battle line moved backwards and forwards only slightly, as first one side and then the other gained the advantage. Whenever the Soviet line was forced back a hurricane of artillery and mortar fire would descend upon the Grenadiers. Little batches of men fought for isolated houses throughout those cold days of January and February 1945 but then on 22 February came relief from the line allowing the Grossdeutschland remnants to be rested and reinforced.

Their efforts had not been in vain but had gained time and prevented the Soviet High Command from deploying the forces held around East Prussia on more important sectors of the battle line. The defensive battle had been successful in that the Pillau road had been reopened and that there was, once again, communication between that town and Königsberg. If the losses which Panzer Grenadier Division Grossdeutschland had suffered had been severe those which it had inflicted on the enemy had been far greater and on 16 February the panzer battalion had destroyed twenty-one of the Soviet machines.

On St David's Day the main of the division was back in the deep southern sector of the line and to the old familiar routine. A Soviet assault on 3 March was beaten into the ground but night assaults which 2nd Battalion of the Grenadiers made during the 6th were crushed and beaten back. Supply difficulties and shortages were affecting the defence for by this time the divisional artillery was rationed to twelve rounds per gun per day and nothing was coming forward: neither men, nor machines nor supplies.

The grand assault which began the last offensive of the war on the Eastern Front fell upon the East Prussian Front at the same time as it did all along the line. The seven Soviet armies on the right wing of the Soviet force were determined to reduce those stubborn pockets of German resistance which still held out. On 13 March, line after line of Red infantry, came in behind a barrage of such proportion that many who experienced it have described it in the one word 'apocalyptic' – trying to express the earth-quaking shock of the super heavy artillery shells, the heat, the smoke, the flames and the sense of utter despair which they felt. Theirs was the realisation that in such a bombardment there could be no square inch of ground that would not be torn open by shell, bomb or rocket and the belief that death was only inches or seconds away. Yet there were soldiers who survived the holocaust and rose up out of their shattered trenches to man the parapets with machine-guns and rocket launchers ready to engage the armour and infantry which now came towards them at the charge. Where the weight of the Soviet pressure forced back the German line then counter-attack units stormed forward determined to regain the lost ground with nothing but their bravery and ability to match the overwhelming Soviet material superiority.

For the next four days the battle raged but then at dawn on 17 March Soviet armour broke through and struck for the sea. A lone Tiger tank – only three now remained from the entire 3rd Panzer Battalion – moved out to engage the waves of T.34s, KVs and Stalin tanks which ranged across the countryside. It did not live long. Under the pressure of armour and infantry on the ground and assault from the air the whole German line was forced back and the town of Brandenburg given up. There was bitter fighting in the woods around Schölen; battles to hold back the closely pursuing Soviet infantry for the orders were that the line must hold to allow time for the German civilians to be evacuated. Slowly, under tremendous pressure the Grossdeutschland remnants were pushed further and further back into the Balga peninsula, south-west of Königsberg, and in the fighting there the last two Tiger tanks went down battling against an armada of Red machines.

Slowly during March the line pulled back and then with the realisation they could retreat no more and that their backs were quite literally to the sea, the Germans opened the sluices and flooded the land halting the Red Army's tank thrusts.

Final positions were dug along a line near Kahlholz in the northern point of the Balga peninsula and all the troops in the area passed under Grossdeutschland command. OKW then decided that the specialist abilities of Grossdeutschland should not be wasted holding a bridgehead in that remote peninsula and orders came for the division to evacuate. During the night of 29th the battalions moved silently down the steep bluffs of Kahlholz to the waiting ferries while on the cliff top 562nd Division held the outpost line to cover the retreat. When the Soviet assault came in this perimeter group died to a man.

Shortly after midnight the 'Seasnake', the name given to the strange collection of ferries, steamed away. Those who left Balga and who disembarked in Samland – the small area of East Prussia between the Kurisch and the Frische Haff – could no longer be called a division for they lacked heavy weapons and equipment. They were a remnant. The panzer men having no longer any tanks and the recce battalion being now without armoured vehicles, all entered the battle as infantrymen whenever the cry came for counter-attack units to storm forward. OKW's intent to retain Grossdeutschland for more vital tasks could not be realised; there was nothing now that could prevent the destruction of Germany. Königsberg, which Grossdeutschland had defended so stoutly and so bloodily, fell on 9 April. Four days later, having regrouped its forces, Stavka opened the final thrust against the remnants of the German Army still holding out in East Prussia.

The men of Grossdeutschland had not been soldiers for years without having acquired some old soldiers' tricks and through scrounging they had assembled a small number of heavy weapons, artillery only, for there was in any case no petrol for vehicles. Armed with these, Grossdeutschland, though not as mobile as it once had been, was again able and capable. Teams of tank busters went out to seek and to destroy the Soviet armoured fighting vehicles which penetrated the front line.

The bombardments which preceded the Soviet infantry assaults on 13 April were frightful in their power. Into the fight were thrown aircraft of every type supporting the hundred regiments of Red artillery, ranging in type from field to siege and all this effort was against thin lines of men holding a narrow strip of East Prussian soil. As the bombardment continued divisional battle groups moved to jump-off positions behind the front line. From those points their counter-attacks would begin to drive back the Soviet infantry which would come flooding in once the barrage had ended.

The Soviet infantry charged unexpectedly quickly through the German front catching off guard groups of Grossdeutschland men and the detachments of other experienced soldiers who were moving forward to engage them.

Here and there a detachment of Grenadiers, a handful of men around a machine-gun, would hold a position; at some other point a team of tank busters would throw themselves into battle against the waves of Soviet tanks thrusting towards Pillau, the last harbour in German hands. The German groups carried out their own attacks without any sort of direction, the junior commanders deciding for themselves the objectives and intentions of their moves. All their efforts were directed towards holding Pillau from whose quays and harbour boats loaded to the gunwales with refugees and wounded dodged the water spouts of the Soviet bombardment.

The remaining Grossdeutschland detachments concentrated in the area north of Polennen and organised a purely infantry defence for there was no longer any artillery. Against this thin, unsupported but defiant line a new Soviet storm broke during the afternoon of 15 April. The area in which the Panzer Grenadier Division was to fight its last battles as an organised body was a long and narrow peninsula near whose point lay Pillau and beyond this again a canal separating the peninsula from a small appendix of land – the Kobbelhude.

It was to protect Pillau that the remnants of the division fought so hard and so desperately during the succeeding weeks of battle. The fighting no longer formed a coherent whole for it was carried out by small bodies, which went down in the fighting and whose heroism has gone unrecorded. Small counter-attack groups led by officers, NCOs and even Grenadiers struck back at Soviet thrusts and in some of these engagements there was support from German warships or naval coastal batteries in position along the peninsula. Slowly the line was taken back until, during the night of 15 April, Pillau itself was threatened and the fighting troops began to cross the narrow strip of water which separated the main length of the peninsula from the appendix at Kobbelhude. A daring Soviet thrust that night captured many Grossdeutschland men awaiting evacuation but other detachments of the division which had managed to escape immediate capture, fought on in buildings and in the ruins of houses. They were, in truth, only postponing the inevitable but they were determined to hold out to the last.

Even those soldiers which landed in the little appendix of land found that their move had been anticipated by the Soviets who had carried out an assault landing from the sea.

During 29 April, fresh orders instructed the remnants of the Panzer Grenadier Division Grossdeutschland – only a few hundred men by this time – to evacuate to Hela, another peninsula near Danzig, an intermediate stage to their final destination of Bornholm, a Danish island in the Baltic. The rearguard of the division reached the island during the night of 3/4 May but even on Bornholm there was no escape from the Soviets and another sea journey brought the little groups to the town of Flensburg in Denmark. There, on 9 May, the men from the Samland fighting passed into British captivity. The Panzer Grenadier Division Grossdeutschland, for months past no longer a division in anything but name and spirit, passed into the greyness of barbed-wire enclosures and the anonymity of prisoner of war camps. It was all over.

Headquarters Panzer Corps Grossdeutschland and Panzer Grenadier Division Brandenburg in the battles along the Oder, January-May 1945

The Soviet attack which burst out of the Baranov bridgehead during the morning of 13 January struck most severely the 4th Panzer Army and the southern wing of 9th Army. Despatched by Hitler to close the gaps which had been torn in the German front and to cut off the rampaging Soviet tank spearheads, the Headquarters of Panzer Corps Grossdeutschland, together with the Panzer Grenadier Division Brandenburg and 1st Division of the Herman Göring Panzer Corps were sent southwards and reached their given destination, the city of Lodz, during the night of 16/17 January, where fresh orders directed them upon Kutno. The length of front that these formations had to hold extended over 60km and, the weakness of the German formations allowed only a thin line of outposts behind which was a small counter-attack reserve.

The speed of the Soviet advance was frightening. The Red Army tank men had adopted and had adapted the original concepts of *blitzkrieg* and were applying the lessons of this warfare against the originators on a scale that left the Germans completely bewildered.

For a German unit to be unprepared was for it to die; a lesson which was learnt by 2nd Battalion of 2nd Jäger Regiment. It had detrained and moved out towards Petrikau where it was to billet for the night. The sounds of battle should have warned its commanders but they, trusting in the defence put up by other units, took no special precautions. The Soviet tank spearheads broke through and rolled over the whole battalion. All the battalion's equipment, heavy weapons and most of its men were lost. Quickly the regiment closed front and formed a skirmish line which was pushed back towards Lodz. This was now part of the forward combat zone and through it rumbled the self-propelled vehicles of the Grossdeutschland Corps, en route to the front to bring forward an advance which had already been halted along the whole front as the German command's counter-attacks were flung back by the strong Soviet forces advancing from captured Warsaw.

As the Jäger Groups arrived they were taken straight from the trains in which they had been travelling and marched up the line. Two companies of Brandenburg were all that could be spared from the now weakened regiment and the defence of Kutno depended chiefly upon about 280 men of the Jäger Regiment and a handful of *Volkssturm*.

Barely had the men of Brandenburg companies settled down than at about 20.00hr on the evening of 18 January, the first probing assault came in to establish the strength of the defence and to discover weak points along its front.

That first weak and hesitant thrust was easily driven off, but tanks with high velocity cannon brought down the houses which the Brandenburg Jäger were holding. From windows and doors there were sheets of flame as rocket launchers were fired at the column of T.34s which swept down a main street firing as they advanced. One T.34 then another, a third tank and a fourth halted burning in the street but the remainder of the point unit broke through and behind these came other vehicles carrying Red Army infantry. The Jäger who had survived now knew that their time had come. There were too many enemy and their own numbers were so few. The choice was stark; retreat or die. They withdrew.

The whole front of Panzer Corps Grossdeutschland was now a series of isolated groups heading back towards the river Warthe, the only barrier which might stem the Soviet advance. There was no contact between Corps HQ and its constituent units nor, indeed, was there any between the individual units of Brandenburg Division. There may have been no wireless or telephone communication but with lightning speed the word went round the scattered units 'Make for the Warthe, the Division is holding bridgeheads there'.

The initial shock of the Soviet assault had now passed and attempts were being made to establish some sort of order out of the chaos caused by that first massive blow. Already divisional or corps units were holding crossing places – bridges and fords across the rivers and streams over which the withdrawing German forces would have to pass. Orders from Corps HQ sent in the SPs to guard the rear of the Brandenburg forces. The self-propelled artillery fought the whole day long with Soviet tank units and Cossack cavalry patrols which had filtered through the forests. Towards last light they arrived at the Gabria bridges with fuel tanks empty of petrol and ammunition racks empty of shells. There was little that the German forces – scattered and lacking heavy artillery – could do to halt the mass of Soviet tanks which threatened the Gabria river bridge.

It was a race between the Germans and the Soviets to see who would first enter the town of Skieratz and Red armour poured down the road overhauling Jäger units on the march, SPs towing other armoured vehicles and worn out tanks moving slowly down the road back into Germany. There was one consolation for the endangered troops; the bridge across the Narev river towards which all the Grossdeutschland Panzer Corps units were now moving was held and held in strength by the Brandenburg Engineer Battalion. It was into the bridgehead held by that unit that at noon on 22 January the first elements of the division and then Grossdeutschland Corps made contact.

The scene on the Warthe bridge was one of undisciplined panic. Streams of traffic, four or five columns abreast, tried to move across under aerial bombardment. The jams lasted for hours and movement by the trucks was measured in only metres. The vehicles and train of five divisions were attempting to flee the Soviet spearheads. For the German infantry the task was made more simple: the river was frozen and columns of men made their way across the river's frozen surface and on to the safety of the western bank, while behind them on the eastern bank a small perimeter made up of Brandenburg men held back the storming Soviets.

While those defenders of the Warthe bridge were fighting their unequal battle other Soviet units were bypassing this obstacle. By 23 January the first Soviet tanks had captured Oppeln and established a firm position on the Oder's eastern bank. The city of Breslau was threatened.

The front of 4th Panzer Army and 9th Army was gaping wide and no co-ordinated German defence existed except for the marching pocket of the two corps and part of a Brandenburg Jäger Regiment which together with a few SP guns all headed westwards. There developed then one of these incidents of war which are stranger than fiction: units from both armies – the Soviet and the German – were striking for the same target. The Germans in the hope of reaching the safety of the western bank of the Oder and the Soviets in the hope of cutting the Germans off. Speed was the most important factor and neither side had time to engage in fighting. Thus vehicle columns of both armies advanced along parallel roads often within firing distance of each other and each unwilling to halt, deploy and take offensive action against the other. Of course, where the roads crossed there was heavy and bitter fighting for possession. If the Germans arrived first a hasty screen of anti-tank guns, SPs and Jäger armed with rocket launchers would form a rearguard to hold back the Soviet drive. Should the Red Army have reached the junction first then the German column would be met with a pak front backed with massed tanks and then there would be the need to swing round the enemy-held point. Where the lie of the land did not permit deployment of the panzer and armoured personnel carriers then the Jäger would be brought forward to clear the obstacle with infantry attack.

The pattern repeated itself continuously. Hours of waiting in a fever of impatience until a road block had been cleared, then a fast advance until the next halt which might be occasioned by the breakdown of an armoured fighting vehicle across the highway or a group of vehicles destroyed in one of the almost incessant air raids. Traffic moved so slowly that to foot march would have been quicker but there burned within all the drivers the belief that once past the next block it would be a clear road into the German lines and back to safety.

On 26 January, when the Brandenburg and Grossdeutschland Corps HQ units crossed the German frontier, the tempo did increase as the vehicle columns roared up the main road towards the Oder and safety. Once again it was the traffic of five German divisions which was using the highway but now traffic control was enforced, where necessary by pistols, to keep the flow moving.

However fast may have been the withdrawal of the German troops, the advance of Koniev's troops had been even quicker and the Soviet perimeters which had first established on 24 January had been built up and expanded to a point where a small but solid foothold existed on the western bank of the river near Koben. Already their aggressive patrols were moving into the open country testing the strength of the German defence. For the Army Group this was another serious crisis which had to be overcome, and it was a matter of prime importance that this threat be removed and quickly. One Panzer group west of the Oder was given that task while others were set against the area east of the river and the enemy forces which were gathered in strength in the great bend of the Oder.

Along the whole front only Grossdeutschland Corps, it was believed, had the strength. Orders then went out for it to swing southwards to attack the Soviet units in the Oder bend and to help smash the Köbenbridgehead. This was a task beyond the capabilities of the corps and one which could only have succeeded against an enemy thin on the ground and weakly positioned whereas the Soviets had had more than a week to prepare their field fortifications. Against an enemy in firm positions and strong in number the best efforts of the Grossdeutschland Corps were to be in vain. The first assault moved off in brilliant moonlight and made good ground seizing footholds across some minor rivers. The Soviet outer defence fell back upon the main line.

Fighting was once again at point-blank range with the German artillery firing over open sights against the T.34s. Burning houses shone on the snow and illuminated the Jäger as they struggled forward against heavy opposition.

But the whole effort had been pointless and orders came for the group to pull back – the divisional attack had been cancelled and a withdrawal had been ordered to the Oder.

The units concentrated and rested out of the line but then came the order that the Red Army's bridgehead at Köben which had so far resisted all attempts to reduce it, was to be the division's next objective.

The Reconnaissance Battalion struck the enemy during the course of 1 February and was followed by an attack on the following day. Both Jäger battalions were put into the attack to gain the town of Mlitsch. But first the dominant hill outside the town, Point 141, had to be taken. The terrain was unsuitable for an unsupported infantry attack – the first bound was across flat and open country – and to support the Jäger assault SPs and anti-tank guns on SP chassis were brought forward.

The opening attack by the 1st Battalion was made at first light and silently without any barrage. Surprise was complete, the companies gained considerable ground and it seemed as if the objectives would be gained but then the 2nd Battalion ran into determined, fanatical opposition and lost one third of its men within a few hours. The armoured vehicles rolled forward to flank the Soviet opposition and attack it from the rear thus releasing pressure upon 2nd Battalion but the Red Army Command had anticipated the move and, as the panzer roared and crunched their way across the snow covered fields to reach a crossroads north of Mlitsch, they came under attack from a column of Red tanks in superior strength and supported by infantry. The fighting throughout the day was hard but indecisive. The Grossdeutschland Corps Commander realised that a resumption of his attack on the next day would be hardly likely to gain ground unless he could receive massive and immediate support, but this he knew would not be forthcoming. Attacks along the whole battle line were pre-occupying the planners at OKW and true to Hitler's dictum. 'The Eastern Front will have to help itself', the Brandenburg soldiers would have to rely upon their own resources. These proved insufficient when, in the first hour of the night, at 01.00hr on 3 February, a sudden and heavy attack by twenty vehicles of a Soviet tank and infantry group rolled over the Brandenburg line.

There had been no warning as the front line positions were stormed by the assault troops of the Red Army infantry. These had come up out of the snow stabbing and slashing with entrenching tools and close combat weapons, silently and bloodily destroying the men in the forward trenches. Then, with the forward positions in their hand they had moved on towards the houses in which the remainder of the companies were resting and had destroyed them with bomb and explosive charges. With a passage cleared through part of the Brandenburg line the T.34s had come forward, the Red infantry had boarded these and the advance had continued into the rear areas of the Brandenburg units.

By now the front was awake and the drill used in such situations was carried out. The infantry took up all round positions in the houses or villages which they held, while out at the crossroads the anti-tank gunners waited quietly for the first appearance of the Red Army tank wave. Behind the anti-tank gun line the SPs were positioned ready to swing into action and strike at the flanks of the Red advance. Then dark against the white of the snow were the outlines of the Soviet machines and carried on the strong wind the rattling of tracks as these squeaked and whistled through the deep snow. Fire was opened at close range and the duel between the Soviet tanks and the German anti-tank gunners was brief and costly. Seven of the Red Army's vehicles lay wrecked or burning while two of the German guns lay silent. The tank wave swept on through the Brandenburg positions heading always westwards; the instructions to the Soviet tank men was still the same – gain ground.

Orders had by now come into Corps HQ that the halted attack upon Mlitsch be resumed and the Jäger Battalions moved through the thick forests, almost unopposed, reached a main road which ran east of the deep woods and cut it. Supply columns nourishing the Soviet spearhead were intercepted, bombarded and destroyed or turned back.

For the whole of 3 February and for greater part of 4th the Jäger companies held their positions, fighting back the counter-attacks which were launched against them, but during 4th came the realisation that they were now completely cut off – a small island of resistance miles behind the Soviet front. Exposed on either flank and with no firm line to the rear along which to withdraw, there could be only one decision if the units were to remain a fighting force. Reluctantly the Jäger moved back across the ground which they had fought so hard to gain and in their rearward movement were harried the whole time by swarms of Cossack cavalry, motorised assaults and bombardment from field and heavy artillery.

The Brandenburg men did not give ground willingly and heavy fighting took place as they turned at bay to hold back the onrushing pursuers. One village was considered important enough by both sides to be fought for so heavily that possession of it changed hands three times during one day. Slowly the Jäger pulled back taking casualties the whole time but inflicting upon the Red infantry more than they suffered. One particularly heavy attack during 8 February came in against 1st Battalion of 2nd Regiment holding a line south of Raudten. Preceded by a shell barrage from those of the lightest to the heaviest calibre the Red Army infantry and tanks swarmed forward to the assault. The infantry were not the front line combat troops but men of a second or third wave. They had no white camouflage suits to conceal them and their brown uniforms made them distinctive against the white background of the snowy expanses which they crossed. They fell in bunches as the men of 1st Battalion opened fire upon these clearly defined targets. With great determination the Soviet infantry pressed forward, their lines becoming looser and looser as the concentrated machine-gun fire of the Brandenburg defenders tore great gaps in their formation.

Across the snow the sound of cheering came, the long drawn out 'Oooray' of the Soviet charge, heard faintly above the noise of the machine-guns. Gallantly the brown line of Soviet infantry pushed through the fire but less than a hundred metres before the Jäger positions the last survivors of this human wave collapsed and died or began to withdraw, wading across the snow with their regiments shattered and flung back.

On other parts of the Brandenburg line, however, the furious assaults had broken into the Jäger defences and house to house fighting took place in 2nd Battalion's area. The fighting for possession of the houses in Polach was bitter and the line moved backwards and forwards as first one side and then the other gained the advantage. Although in the Brandenburg sector the Soviet advance was being held, even if with considerable difficulty, at other points along the German line, units were being forced back and in their rearward movement were exposing the flanks of the Panzer Corps. Through these gaps between the flank of Brandenburg and the neighbouring division there now poured a flood of Red Army men and vehicles, bypassing the opposition put up by the Jäger battalions, leaving them to be dealt with by follow-up troops. These obstinate German units were now so severely reduced in number that one company numbered six men and a sergeant, but they were still determined to resist and only upon orders did they withdraw from the positions which they had held in and around Polach.

The determined defence put up by the Grossdeutschland Corps and its constituent units had placed it in jeopardy for the advanced units of the Red Army were now so far westwards of Corps that it was, to all intents, surrounded and cut off from the main German line. A fresh withdrawal would have to be made if it were to remain intact and in the rearguard fighting which marked the course of the succeeding days Brandenburg lost heavily for, however quickly the Grossdeutschland Corps moved, its Red Army opponents were faster. By 10 February it was clear that the group was again completely encircled and isolated.

Once again, as at so many points along the German front, a major battle group prepared to form itself into a hedgehog and to fight its way through to reach its own Army's front line. The fighting in which the Brandenburg units were now involved was no different to that which in the far north of the country Grossdeutschland Panzer Grenadier Division was engaged. The place names were different; the tactics adapted slightly to meet the conditions of terrain, but basically it was a movement by a column of vehicles, protected on either flank by patrols and with an advanced guard and rearguard made up of armour, anti-tank and infantry. Along the journey through enemy-held country there were the assaults by Red Army units to impede the western drive, concentrated barrages, regiments of artillery and Katyushas, road blocks of Red Army pak-fronts, tank assaults and attacks from the air by the Soviet Air Force. During the night of 11th/12th the advanced guard of Grossdeutschland Corps hedgehog made contact with the bridgehead held by Brandenburg Division's Replacement Battalion and the shape of the pocket changed from column into line as Corps HQ the Panzer Grenadier Division Brandenburg and 20th Panzer Grenadier Division – which together had formed the moving pocket – advance on a broad front towards the main German line.

The Grossdeutschland Corps had broken through but it had been a bitter time. The losses in dead, wounded and missing men had been enormous; materially they were appalling and in vehicles disastrous. Militarily the Grossdeutschland Corps had been reduced in fighting strength to less than that of a regiment. Morally, however, the survivors of the battles and of the breakout were still able and they needed to be for the Soviet offensive had still not completely run its course and fresh battles lay ahead of them.

Once back in the main German line Brandenburg and the Grossdeutschland Corps joined in a general withdrawn towards the Neisse river. At a river line the rearguard of Jäger companies would halt and hold position flinging back the first Soviet assaults and gaining time for fresh troops to arrive for new positions and a firm line to be established along which the Soviet drive might at last be halted. Along the river Quies they fought to destroy a Soviet bridgehead and in the woods which ran almost to the river banks there was hand to hand fighting against overwhelming odds. Under such pressure they withdrew on 15th, moving through a countryside in a state of panic at the drive of the Soviet Army.

Along the line of advance which the Soviets would have to take bridges were blown, road curves blown away and extensive minefields laid to slow down the pace of the thrust but none of these had any effect and the Red Army Command crammed on the pressure driving its units forward into the heartland of Germany.

At the Neisse river the Brandenburg Division and the remainder of Panzer Corps Grossdeutschland halted and turned to face their pursuers for one last desperate battle along the 32km of front which they were expected to hold until the last. Suddenly, however, the pressure of the Soviet drive was lessened; the great offensive had finally run out of impetus and along the southern part of the front Soviet troops remained in position on the eastern bank of the Neisse. Further north there was already a Soviet bridgehead on the western bank of the Oder but this too, like the positions in front of Grossdeutschland Corps, was to stay dormant until the last great drive by the Red Army in April which was to capture Berlin and to play its part in bringing the war in Europe to a close.

The positions which Panzer Corps Grossdeutschland had taken up as a result of the general withdrawal following upon the battles of January and February were expanded and strengthened during the weeks of comparative quiet which elapsed before the last great Soviet offensive during April. The quiet was indeed only comparative for patrols roamed across the Neisse into the Soviet lines, maintaining a Grossdeutschland bridgehead which still existed at Muskau on the river's eastern bank and striking back at the Red Army patrols which tried to cross into the divisional territory.

Deeply conscious of the terrible weakness of their own armies, knowledgeable of how deep inside Germany were the approaching Western Allies but yet determined to go down fighting, the men of Brandenburg and of Panzer Corps HQ spent the weeks in preparing for defence. Every village was fortified, houses were turned into strong points, church towers became observation points and minefields laid across the obvious paths of advance. Throughout February and for the greater part of March the Jäger dug and prepared a series of defence lines and trained the young men of the Hitler Youth in the tactics of close quarter tank destruction.

On the Soviet side there had been a build-up of men and weapons. From the factories and from the homeland of the Soviet peoples the arms and the machines were produced and the trained reserves brought forward to the Oder/Neisse line. Tank divisions lay concealed in the great woods east of the rivers; engineers had prepared bridging equipment to speed the advance; and, to cover the first infantry assaults, masses of guns and the shells to fire shattering barrages had been positioned. The strength of the Soviet armies opposite the Grossdeutschland sector grew rapidly during the weeks of waiting.

German staff appreciations established that the main force of the Soviet blow along the Neisse would fall in the area of Rothenburg and to meet this threat the Panzer Grenadier Division Brandenburg was moved, from those well-established positions which it had dug, southwards to be placed as a block in the path of the imminent Soviet offensive. The new sector which the division occupied ran from Wehrkirch to Stembach and covered the approaches to the Silesian industrial area. In order to meet the first Soviet thrusts with the maximum strength both regiments were put into the line. Recruits, the last reinforcements, volunteers all, that were to be received by the division, filled out the companies – convalescents returned to their units to fight with the division in its final battle. Every depot, every training establishment and every military school in Germany formed its men and staff into battle groups and sent them up the line to hold the eastern wall. All that could be prepared had been made ready.

There was increased activity on the part of the Red Air Force; fresh regiments of artillery shot themselves in; *panje* carts in long columns drove along narrow forest paths bringing to the most advanced artillery and mortar positions the ammunition which was to destroy the German defences; and crack Red Army troops crammed into the infantry's front line trenches.

On Sunday 16 April, an intelligence appreciation from Grossdeutschland Corps HQ issued to all units under its command, warned that the Soviet offensive was to begin on the following day. The Brandenburg bridgehead at Muskau was evacuated.

Even before the great barrage began Red Army assault pioneers had tried to erect bridges across the shallow, 15m-wide Neisse river, and despite counter-attacks by the Brandenburg Jäger Companies the Soviets had, by evening, erected a primitive but sturdy erection and the first Red Army assault infantry had forced the river bridgehead. Attempts by Jäger companies to fling back the Army infantry failed to turn back the Red Army men. All that the Jäger could do was to seal off the penetration area and hope to bring up strong forces during the night so that at dawn the incursions could be flung back.

In the dark of the night the fighting died down; the artillery fire began to lessen and then stopped altogether. In an hour midnight would end Sunday and bring in Monday 16 April; D-Day for the Soviet assault. At 15.00hr the 1st Ukrainian Front, whose armies and divisions stood opposite the sector held by the Grossdeutschland Corps, opened its main assault with a three-hour-long barrage from hundreds of guns, thousands of Katyushas and other mortars. The initial bombardment smashed trenches and strong points, destroying the carefully constructed positions and killing the Jäger who had manned the front line. It was upon the sector held by the 2nd Jäger Regiment's 1st Battalion that the full fury of the Soviet blow fell and all organised resistance ceased in that area. The few surviving Jäger looking over the edge of their slit trenches could see advancing towards them long lines of Red Army infantry, stretching for miles on either side of their positions and leading the assault waves were columns of tanks.

The massive Soviet thrust burst out of the bridgehead in which it had been contained and having crashed through the 1st Battalion swung northwards to roll up the Brandenburg line, expanding its front as it moved and driving before it the few Jäger who had survived the fury of the bombardment.

The defensive plans which had been laid by the Grossdeutschland Corps staff had little significance now; nor did the small ad hoc groups hastily assembled and put into positions to hold the Soviet forward flow have any success. As fast as the groups opened fire and betrayed their position then down upon them would fall the fury of the Soviet armoured thrust and they would be blown apart by gunfire and by the T.34s which swarmed across the country.

It would be unfair to say that the Soviet advance was everywhere completely uncontested. Small groups, even individuals who took up the fight, fired at the T.34s as they rolled past, destroying them with *Panzerfaust* or with explosive charges. Down in the bridgehead area small groups of Brandenburg Jäger had formed themselves into counter-attack forces and were striking back at the masses of Red Army infantry crossing the Neisse. Soviet reports of the battle speak of men of 58th Guards Division, impatient at the delay to their advance, wading across the river holding their weapons above their heads while men from other units were floating themselves across on pieces of wood, tree trunks…on anything that would float and carry their weight.

Against one counter-attack, which a hastily assembled Tiger group in company strength had begun to make, the Soviets with their infinitely greater numbers detached a battalion and it was this imbalance and superiority at every point which allowed them to move further and further westwards, striking on a narrow front with a great concentration of power, intent upon gaining ground. The Soviet armoured group had by now divided with one column striking northwards and the other westwards following the practices of *blitzkrieg* by avoiding resistance and striking deep into the rear areas of Brandenburg's sector. Behind these columns there poured a flood of infantry which covered the ground and seemed to be everywhere at once.

By midday some sort of cohesive defence had been formed and a counter-attack was launched by the Jäger regiments and the Engineer Battalion of the Brandenburg Division. As the Soviets advanced they encountered stiffer opposition and at places the Brandenburg units went over to counter-attacks driving back the Red infantry and out of some of the villages which they had captured. To support the Jäger and the engineers in their unequal battle a regiment of anti-aircraft guns with 88mm weapons came under command and for the next few days were the backbone of the determined resistance which the Panzer Corps HQ and its units maintained.

By last light on Monday 16th, it was clear, however, that the Soviets had broken through the divisional front and had created a breach about 8km wide and had penetrated to a depth of about 15km. Along the walls of the salient many of the local attacks by the Brandenburg units were achieving very little for no co-ordinated defence or attack could be mounted as there was neither wireless nor telephone communication between Corps headquarters and its subordinate units. Emergency measures were taken. Certain reorganisations had become essential, 1st Battalion of 1st Regiment had been placed under command of 2nd Regiment to build up that unit's strength after the loss of its own first battalion. But there was little else which could be done, there were no reserves and the orders to all the troops on the Eastern Front had been the same, 'There will be no withdrawal; no retreat.' Yet unless there was an immediate adjustment and the front was withdrawn then encirclement and destruction were certain.

Throughout the night of 17 Arpil, the Brandenburg officers used their best endeavours to group the fragments of their units into a whole and to form new defence lines along which to hold the next day's assaults by the Soviet forces. The fate of the Brandenburg Division, and with it the whole Grossdeutschland Panzer Corps, rested upon the individual efforts of the battalion commanders. Their small commands were widely separated. In land around Kodersdorf were grouped the remnants of 2nd Regiment; in the woods each of Hähnichen the fragments of 1st Regiment. A major grouping of the Engineer Battalion, the Divisional Artillery Regiment and the attached Flak Regiment was located in Wehrkirch and the Corps Engineer Battalion was in Sagar.

At dawn on the 17th the Soviet thrusts began again and their first efforts fell upon those survivors of the 2nd Regiment's 1st Battalion which had already suffered so much during the first day of the offensive, and having scattered, the Reds went on to strike at the other units of the division.

Along those sections of the divisional front wherever and whenever determined resistance was encountered the Soviets halted their forward movement and brought the full fury of artillery barrages upon the defenders. At Wehrkirch, where a determined and aggressive defence was maintained by the Divisional Engineers the Flak Regiment and the Divisional Artillery, the Red Artillery bombardment was particularly heavy. The defence of Wehrkirch had been destructive to the Soviet attackers; no less than forty Soviet tanks lay broken or on fire in or around the place, and the strongest efforts were made by the Red Army commanders to seize the town. Under the pressure which the Soviets were exerting there was no military logic in Brandenburg maintaining its hold and, during the early afternoon, orders came to evacuate and to withdraw from shattered and burning Wehrkirch.

Corps intended to take up a new defence line based upon Niesky but so close in pursuit were the Red Army spearheads that after a short but bitter battle that place too was evacuated. Against other sectors of the Corps front Soviet pressure mounted as the three Red Armies – 52nd, the 2nd Polish and the Guard's Army – were regrouped and put back in with orders to smash past the Grossdeutschland defenders. The Soviet westward drive had now brought one pincer arm near the great Dresden *autobahn* while the other had struck for Bautzen. The few and scattered groups of Brandenburg Jäger, with few panzer and supported by the remaining guns, withdrew contesting every yard of the ground with the closely pursuing Soviet troops. Everywhere the Red Army soldiers were exerting pressure, probing, infiltrating, attacking and bombarding their way forward. German resistance in any one place could be measured in hours sometimes and very rarely in days for there was always the knowledge that the Red spearheads were already far to the west and that encirclement was only a matter of time.

At some places the hard-pressed Jäger stood and fought off their pursuers. At Boxberg, for example, the last SP guns of the Grossdeutschland Corps Armoured Artillery Brigade and elements from the Engineer Battalion struck back at one persistent Soviet armoured column. The SPs, firing from carefully selected firing points, began to destroy the Red armour at very long range and as the T.34s scattered under the fire of the high velocity German guns the Assault Engineers came at them with rocket launchers and explosive charges destroying them at close quarters.

Slowly there was a stiffening in the German defence east of Spreefurth, the first impetus of the Soviet assault died away and the elements of Brandenburg and Panzer Corps HQ which were still out of touch with their own headquarters placed thcmselves under the command of neighbouring units whose organisation was still intact. Thus 2nd Jäger Regiment joined with 20th Panzer Division and 1st Regiment with 615 Special Purposes Division. It was together with these other units that the Jäger regiments took part in the series of local German counter-attacks which marked the next few days. One such assault was to be a pincer operation carried out by both 1st and 2nd Regiments striking southwards and northwards respectively against the Soviet salient in the area of Klitten.

At Niesky the staunch defence put up by the Jäger and engineer garrison continued to consume the best efforts of the Red forces. Infuriated by the resistance of this handful of Brandenburg men the local Soviet commanders brought up reinforcements but made the mistake of bringing them to within range of the SPs which were supporting the Jäger. Fire was then turned upon these groups of infantry reinforcement who had been formed up and set against the defence in close column of companies. A barrage of shells from the SPs crashed down upon the packed ranks and before the unfortunate infantry had had time to deploy or to escape from the fury of the barrage they had been nearly all killed and wounded. The Soviet commanders having failed to subdue the Niesky garrison with armour or with infantry then brought up regiments of Cossacks and sent these in at the charge, but under the fire of the MG 42s, handled by men with years of experience, the galloping squadrons were cut down in swathes. *Panzerfaust* were used to blow apart the cavalry units as they bunched in the narrow streets. Across the bodies of the dead and dying more infantry attacks came in but with as little result as the first assaults. At regulated intervals the Red infantry stormed forward, attacking first from one direction, then another and from different directions, but always at the same precise intervals of time. Once the pattern had been established it was easy for the defenders to rush their guns from one threatened place to another and with concentrations of fire to smash into the ground each and every attack.

Niesky was now so far behind the Red front line that its fall was only a matter of time and to avoid the total destruction of the Brandenburg garrison it was ordered to withdraw from the town and to rejoin the main body of the division. The breakout was made in the early hours of 21 April and after an adventurous journey contact was made with the German outpost line at Särchen just after dawn.

The survivors of the Niesky garrison were then put in to support the pincer operation which was being mounted by 1st and 2nd Regiments. The 1st Regiment, with which the engineers fought, had advanced so far that it had cut the Red supply route – the Bautzen road – and had gone on to attack other positions in Dauban. The 2nd Battalion of 1st Regiment had also made good progress and had carried out its attack with such force and precision that the Soviet troops in that sector were driven back in confusion and lost a number of tanks, soft-skinned vehicles and other military equipment.

Against the Soviet counter-attacks which then came in the Jäger line stood firm and by accurate machine-gun and mortar fire forced the Soviet infantry to debus from the tanks on which they were riding and to open their attack on foot. As the columns of T.34s moved threateningly towards a crossroads which the Jäger were holding a single Panzer V, a Panther, took up a position on the flank from which it could enfilade the Soviet column and, using a well-tried tactic, began to destroy the tanks one after the other. The long 75mm gun in the Panther fired and destroyed the last tank in the column and the turret swung towards the second from last Soviet vehicle, smashed that one and continued up the line blowing the T.34s apart with its high velocity shells until the whole column had been smashed. With their armoured support destroyed before their eyes the Soviet infantry attack began to falter and then fell back, hastened in their flight by the rapid fire which the Jäger poured upon them.

By now the unexpectedly determined defence put up by the Brandenburg Division and the Grossdeutschland Corps had upset the Soviet timetable in that sector and had deflected from its course the thrust against Dresden which Stavka had intended should be made by 1st Ukrainian Front. To bypass the strong resistance which the division was still putting up the Soviet effort swung north towards Berlin but to maintain pressure upon the Brandenburg front the Soviet Command put in elite guards divisions.

During 25/26 April, Brandenburg was ordered to re-capture the town of Bautzen which had fallen to a determined Soviet thrust – and possession of which was held by Army Group Centre to be of great importance to the continuation of a successful defence by Grossdeutschland Corps east of Dresden. The offensive which the division was now to undertake was nothing less than an attempt to amputate one of the major Soviet spearheads. To add strength to the Branden-burg operation, elements of both 20th and 21st Panzer Divisions were to be committed. The opening of the offensive augured well but with every passing hour the resistance put up by the Soviets and by the Poles of the 1st Ukrainian Front grew stronger and counter-attacks were launched against the Jäger regiments struggling to bring the assault forward.

The front line Red Army units had absorbed the full brunt of the Brandenburg drive and lost heavily. At one place the Soviet defenders of Casslau lost fifteen tanks in as many minutes, but the pace of the German forward movement slowed and was then halted as Stavka brought more and more men into the battle. The infusion of these fresh troops turned the tide. Under attack by aircraft, by tanks and by infantry, bombardment from the ground and from the air the assault troops of the Jäger regiments withdrew slowly, returning at times to the attack to regain a lost position, the recapture of which could be of only brief duration. One such attack was ordered for 29 April but then the Jäger regiments were relieved from the line and were moved from the Neisse river sector. With this move they were not only to leave that area of the front but thereby to come under the command of another Army Group and, therefore, out of the control of Grossdeutschland Panzer Corps.

The area into which the Brandenburg Division now moved in those first days of May was Czechoslovakia where the last organised defence by German units was still being maintained and it was in the town of Olmütz that the units were detrained and put into position along the northern flank of Schörner's Army Group. The task of the division was to guard Army Group's left wing as it moved slowly back towards Germany. The remainder of the division formed a protective line to guard the rear of the Army Group, fighting desperately against the masses of Red Army infantry and tanks, which were trying to cut off this last island of resistance.

This was, however, now almost at an end. The death of Hitler in the ruins of Berlin, the armistice in Italy and the full knowledge that the Allies were in possession of most of the German homeland led to a weakening of resistance and desertion by some units from the line through which the Soviet infantry and armour advanced.

The hope of an organised withdrawal through Czech territory back into Germany completely faded. The Jäger units fighting in and around Olmütz were still holding their positions and battling against the tanks and artillery with which the Soviets were hoping to achieve a total breakthrough and then on 8 May they began their own rearward movement with the intention of breaking through to the Bavarian Forest.

The road back into Germany was completely blocked with vehicles, refugees, horses and carts and all the paraphernalia of a retreating army. Only at pistol point could the road be cleared of the obstructions which impeded the advance and the Brandenburg vehicles, loaded only with men and their most essential equipment, drove through the night. Everywhere there were signs of dissolution, of Czech partisan activity and road blocks which forced the columns into one diversion after the other. The column halted and this stop lasted longer than the others. Those at the front of the column knew the reason; ahead of them in the little town of Deutschbrod there were Soviet tanks. The Soviet spearheads had cut them off. There could now be no breakthrough to the west and into Germany, for the presence of the Red armour in Deutschbrod showed that other units would have already cut every road back into Germany. There was no possibility of evasion; individuals might succeed in filtering through the Soviet lines but for the Panzer Grenadier Division Brandenburg, as a complete unit, the war which they had fought for years ended – not with a Wagnerian climax in battle but at a crossroads in Bohemia.

Seven

Major Units which formed part of the Grossdeutschland Establishment: Brandenburg and Kurmark

The Panzer Grenadier Division Brandenburg

Perhaps the most interesting but least known formations fielded by the German Army during the Second World War were those known by the title Brandenburg for in their original conception they represented Germany's first, formal attempt to organise units whose specific role it would be to seize strategic targets such as bridges, to infiltrate enemy lines and penetrate the enemy's rearguard areas, to commit sabotage, create confusion or foment revolt. The fundamental difference between Brandenburg and other assault groups was that they would begin their operations *before* an operation was launched, for it was considered that thereby their missions would have a greater chance of being successful and that this success would speed the advance of the follow-up forces, could guarantee a favourable outcome to a specific enterprise and might even influence a whole campaign. To assist them Brandenburg men might be partially disguised in the uniform of their enemy, if necessary.

The short life of the Brandenburg formations covers a rise from ad hoc detachments via a formal establishment in company strength whose true identity was concealed under a cover name, through regimental to divisional status. There then followed the amalgamation of the division with that of Grossdeutschland to form the Panzer Corps Grossdeutschland.

The German Army has, generally, failed to produce the type of soldier successful in partisan or guerrilla operations, the only two notable exceptions being General Paul von Lettow-Vorbeck in East Africa or Wassmuss in the Middle East. The German military mind had perhaps seen something repugnant in *france-tireur* operations and in men who fight in such unconventional situations.

Influenced by the British Army's success against the Turks in Palestine during the First World War, a number of former German colonial officers, friends and colleagues of Admiral Wilhelm Canaris, head of the German intelligence organisation, *Abwehr,* proposed to him that secret, highly mobile and skilfully led groups be raised by the German forces to undertake similar operations against countries with whom Germany might be involved in war. The ideas were acted upon and some time late in 1938, or early in 1939, the first volunteers were interviewed.

Most sources agree that the most probable reason for the raising of Brandenburg units was to seize and thus prevent damage to the Silesian factories which would be among the Army's first objectives in any war waged by the Third Reich against Poland. A second and more subtle reason has also been suggested. Admiral Canaris was a well-known opponent of the Nazi regime and it is believed decided to form a unit of men unswervingly loyal to him who could, if the time came carry out a coup d'etat and overthrow Hitler's government.

Whatever the reason may have been it is certain that, before the Polish campaign opened, the *Abwehr* had formed lightly armed battle groups of Polish-speaking Germans ready to take the field and to move into the Polish factories. Some of these detachments actually entered Poland several days before the declaration of war; other groups followed only hours ahead of the official violation of the frontier by the German Army and the swift action of both groups prevented any acts of sabotage.

As Nazi Germany was located in the heart of Europe it perhaps, understandable that her leaders saw her as rounded by a ring of enemies to combat whom required Brandenburg battle groups staffed by agents with language fluencies. Discreet enquiries for men with such qualifications brought forward a number of native volunteers and others from expatriate Germans who had returned home on the outbreak of war. These men brought with them colloquial knowledge of foreign languages, customs and everyday life but, more important still, up to date official documents, passports, identity cards and ration books with the correct cancellation stamps. These loyal, linguistically capable, adventurous men, together with the local volunteers, were sufficient in number to form first one and then a second Special Purposes Construction Training Company. The first of the two companies had been distinguished further by the addition of the name The German Company. A collective title was needed for the two companies and they were classified and named as No. 800 Special Purposes Construction Battalion.

Training with live ammunition was intensive and the tactics taught were those of the partisan in the forests and of the urban guerrilla in towns. Great emphasis was laid on all-round ability. The skill to move silently through undergrowth; competence in tracking and in navigation by the stars were all painstakingly mastered. Later during the war other companies were to add to those basic skills other abilities, such as ski-ing, parachuting and watermanship. Tuition was given in the manufacture of explosives from simple and readily available materials. In short nothing was omitted from the training programme which might, at some future date, enable the Brandenburg men to fight and win on any terms.

At the end of this intensive training a Brandenburg soldier could move noiselessly and kill silently. He was a skilled saboteur who could live and, as a result of survival courses, fight in the most primitive conditions and difficult situations. And all this he could do, if necessary, completely alone for there was as much emphasis upon emotional stability as upon physical fitness. Many volunteers were accepted; some fell out or were rejected but those who remained knew that they were members of an elite.

They were not seen in this important role by every military commander. To most German officers the use of uniform as a disguise to deceive the enemy was an abuse which demeaned their own uniform. It is not surprising, therefore, that often when the question of using methods of disguise was first mooted many senior officers refused to employ Brandenburg units and considered the companies to be made up of renegades or even criminals. When such disquieting thoughts came to the ears of the rank and file of the Brandenburg detachments their company commanders impressed upon them that their role was to be that of military specialists, highly trained to carry out daring and single missions for which ordinary troops were neither suitable nor competent. The hostility on the part of many senior commanders lasted, however, for nearly the whole of the unit's life and, paradoxically, the knowledge that highly-placed officers looked upon them with disfavour had the effect of producing within Brandenburg a fierce degree of loyalty and a depth of comradeship between the officers and their men.

It cannot be emphasised too strongly that the Brandenburg were soldiers first, foremost and always and must not under any circumstances be thought of as spies. The *Abwehr* may have been the father of the organisation and did impress the stamp of its own secret personality upon it, but the objectives were usually chosen by the High Command and the tactics of deception worked out within the group selected to undertake the mission and in close liaison with Army units in the immediate area.

It would, however, also be incorrect to consider Brandenburg, at least in the early years of its life, as an Army formation, for it was raised to serve under *Abwehr* control. Despite the fact that the unit had a military title and the men wore standard German Army uniform Brandenburg was considered, until late in 1942 to be a uniformed branch of the intelligence services and thus outside of purely military control. Only when the political struggle for control of the intelligence organisation was lost by the *Abwehr* and won by the *Sicherheitsdienst* of the SS did Brandenburg lose this status and cease to operate the type of mission which Canaris had envisaged. Thus, by 1944, the type of operation which was undertaken was no longer the strategic and imaginative thrust mounted by specialists, but the misuse of these highly trained and dedicated men as infantry, fighting within the Panzer Grenadier Division Brandenburg or else serving in anti-partisan operations.

The companies and individual platoons which had been selected to serve in the spring and summer campaigns of 1940, trained in isolation during the winter of 1939/40, reconnoitring the ground of their future operations.

As winter passed into early spring the days began to lengthen – campaigning weather was coming.

The first test of Brandenburg capability was made against Denmark in 1940 when, on 9 April, a platoon dressed in Danish uniform and speaking fluent Danish struck swiftly and silently, captured a strategically important bridge across the Belt and facilitated, thereby, the Army's advance. Other groups went on to strike at targets in Norway.

The focus of military attention was then turned towards the Western Front and once again Brandenburg units were called upon to carry out coup de main operations over a wide area extending from Luxembourg to The Netherlands.

Let us recall the situation facing the German High Command at the start of the campaign. It was of vital importance that within hours of the frontiers being crossed, certain key objectives be gained. Among the principal and vital targets was the fortress of Eben Emael and this was seized in a formal assault executed by glider-landed airborne troops led by the daring Lieutenant Rudolf Witzig of the Para-Engineers, while men of 3rd Battalion of Infantry Regiment Grossdeutschland, carried out the successful air-landing mission, Nivi, behind the Belgian front line. To exploit the favourable situation which these daring operations had achieved and to permit a rapid link-up between the main body of the German Army and the lightly-armed assault troops, obstructions had to be removed along the Luxembourg frontier and a number of bridges across rivers and canals seized to permit the advance of the panzer divisions. All operations to achieve this result were to take place within minutes of each other and many were Braadenburg missions.

There is no room here to describe in detail the actions of each individual group and only the barest outline can be mentioned. Of the four main missions undertaken at the outset of the campaign against France and the Low Countries, let the actions of one group speak for the whole.

Perhaps the most famous, or at any rate, the most audacious operation carried out by a Brandenburg commando during the 1940 campaign was that by men of No. 2 Company against the Gennep bridge in The Netherlands. The need to capture this bridge intact was a vital factor in the Gennan operational plan which required that The Netherlands be overrun within days in order that the northern flank of the panzer advance through Belgium and northern France be covered.

To achieve the quick neutralisation of The Netherlands the river Meuse had to be crossed and held. A number of operations aimed at reaching and obtaining bridgeheads across the river were undertaken; it is the one at Gennep which is of concern to us.

The 150m long Gennep railway bridge lay a little over 5km distant from the German frontier and if it were to be taken before the Dutch could destroy it then the Brandenburg assault group would have to be inside the neutral Netherlands before the campaign had officially opened, if it was to capture the bridge by zero hour. Behind the group, back in Germany, lay two fully loaded troop trains ready to exploit the success and to push on towards and to overrun the main Dutch defences, the Peel position, which lay behind the Meuse. These troop trains were timed to begin their advance precisely at zero hour and were to steam on to and across the bridge which, according to plan, should have been, by that time, seized by the Brandenburg detachment.

The sixty or so men of the Brandenburg group moved into a camp at Asperden which already held a number of Dutch Nazis and there the whole detachment began intensive training for the task which lay ahead.

In order to maintain absolute security the assault group was not selected until the day prior to the outbreak of hostilities and the target was not disclosed to them until they were ready to move into The Netherlands. A nine-man assault commando was chosen.

At 02.00hr on the morning of 10 May the group slipped across the frontier and headed for Gennep railway bridge. Three of the group were disguised as Dutch military police and the other six were in German uniform. By first light they had reached the approach to the bridge and were aware from the noises coming from the German side that the first of the two German troop trains, having crossed the frontier, was approaching Gennep railway station. They had only minutes to capture the bridge intact.

On the Dutch side of the frontier, and in the sudden confusion caused by this unusual activity, the appearance of the nine men on the bridge aroused no suspicion for outwardly it seemed that three fully armed Dutch policemen were escorting six disarmed German soldiers. Each of the 'prisoners' was wearing an unbuttoned overcoat hidden within whose folds and strapped to the chest was a machine pistol. In the overcoat pockets were egg grenades and a pistol. The three 'Dutch' police moved towards the guardhouse on the eastern side of the bridge and as they drew abreast of the unsuspecting Dutch sentries suddenly attacked and overpowered them while the other members of the group began to cut every wire in sight, seeking to destroy not only the telephone connections but also the leads to the explosive charges.

Within a minute the guardroom on the eastern bank was in German hands and then one of the group rang the commander of the guardpost on the west bank and in fluent Dutch told him that a group of German prisoners was coming across the bridge under escort.

The group arrived and was handed over. No search of the 'prisoners' seems to have been undertaken and the Brandenburg men allowed themselves to be removed from the area in a lorry. Behind them on the bridge which the remainder of their unit had now captured the first troop train was crossing and having passed the astonished Dutch sentries, steamed off towards the Peel defensive line.

The 'Captive' Brandenburg group, meanwhile, had escaped from their lorry in the confusion of an air raid, had overpowered their guards, and gone over to the attack, storming pill boxes and taking a haul of forty prisoners.

The success of this brilliantly executed operation at the Gennep bridge was manifested during that day when two German divisions crossed dryshod into The Netherlands.

The end of the campaign against France was not the end of Brandenburg operations in the west, for the United Kingdom was still unconquered and active preparations went ahead for Operation *Sealion*, the invasion of the British Isles. Conventional military plans proposed that the attack take the short sea route to the south-east corner of England and Brandenburg units, their identity concealed under a variety of cover names, were given certain specific tasks to perform in the invasion. Inspired by the brilliant success achieved by Witzig's glider troops at Eben Emael, OKW suggested that a landing be made on the cliffs of Kent, while another Brandenburg group was to undertake a seaborne assault to prevent the sinking of blockships in the mouth of Dover harbour. Yet another group was to storm ashore, as part of an infantry division, between Hastings and St Leonards and was then to head, mounted on special lightweight motor cycles, towards the Royal Artillery coastal batteries on Beachy Head.

In the event Operation *Sealion* was aborted as was a plan to strike at Gibraltar. During the ensuing period of military inactivity the strength of the regiment increased from twelve to seventeen companies, i.e. three battalions, within whose establishment was mustered specialist units and sub-units possessing unusual skills.

The successes gained by Brandenburg units in the two campaigns of 1940 led to the expansion mentioned above and thus a regimental headquarters was required which, in October 1940, formally took over the No. 800 Special Purposes Instruction Regiment Brandenburg.

Despite this regimental grouping individual battalions remained dispersed throughout Germany and even the companies were able to a large degree to remain autonomous, being grouped near to those areas with which their men had a special affinity. The battalions were stationed in Brandenburg in Prussia, in Düren near Aachen and in Baden near Vienna. From these locations it can be seen that each battalion was fitted for operations in a specific area of Europe, and a company was composed of men who spoke the languages and dialects of the countries facing them. As an example the 1st Battalion, stationed in Prussia was made up of the following four companies:

No. 1: Baltic Germans who spoke Latvian, Lithuanian, Estonian, Finnish, Russian or Baltic Russian dialects.
No. 2: Germans from South-east and South-west Africa, speaking Afrikaans, Swahili, native dialects, English and Portuguese.
No. 3: Germans from Sudetenland and from Czechoslovakia speaking Czech and the dialects of Bohemia and Moravia.
No. 4: Germans from Poland speaking Polish, Russian, Ukrainian, Ruthenian and other local dialects.

That simple list gives some idea of the variety of languages which just one battalion commanded. Add to the many tongues and dialects spoken within the whole division, the specialist training which produced a naval assault landing detachment, a parachute battalion, as well as an Alpine unit and some idea can be gained of the wide scope of activities and areas in which the Brandenburg Regiment could be used.

In the spring of 1941, hostilities broke out again when Germany attacked Yugoslavia. On the Danube there is an area, called the Iron Gate, where the river narrows and whoever holds this dictates the movement of shipping along the river. The Danube had to be kept open for German ships and men of 2nd Battalion were airlifted, captured the town of Orshchova and went on to seize the ground on both banks of the river. The Iron Gate was in German hands.

But ahead of the regiment lay the most severely testing time. In June Operation *Barbarossa*, the attack upon the Soviet Union, began.

The great length of the battle line, the few Brandenburg men who were available, the number of vital bridges which needed to be taken and the speed of the subsequent advances have submerged knowledge of Brandenburg operations so that the little which might have been recorded in war diaries was lost in the exultation at the rate of advance or the number of prisoners taken. To select just one from the number of successful missions would be unfair to all the others, but in almost every case the situation was the same. A fast assault in captured lorries by men partly disguised as Soviet soldiers, their discarding of the Soviet uniforms once the objective had been seized and then the strain waiting for relief while around the small, German perimeter, waves of Red Army troops and vehicles struck to annihilate the enemy who had gained a foothold. Such fighting, for the most part unrecorded and unhonoured, formed the life of the Brandenburg units in those first days of fighting.

It was only when the time of the first great advances had passed and the front had, more or less, stabilised that the role of the Brandenburg units changed. One special action was a long range penetration in 1942, when a type of Polar expedition complete with huskies and ski-troops was assembled and posted in Finland. After acclimatisation the operation to destroy the Murmansk railway line was undertaken. An approach march of more than 200km was carried out through a wooded but watery wilderness of oppressive loneliness.

The railway line was reached and a small commando placed explosive devices at widely spaced intervals along the track. The subsequent explosions derailed many supply trains and occasioned a panic in the Red Army's Northern Command HQ.

For the other battalions of Brandenburg there was no opportunity to demonstrate their special aptitudes in the regular fighting on the Eastern Front. Instead they were drawn at first only by groups then by companies and finally as entire battalions, into anti-partisan operations. In order to put into action the strongest possible combination units were expanded in number, sometimes to twice their war establishment figure and were equipped with weapons normally on issue only at regimental level. In fact a beginning had been made to integrate the semi-autonomous detachments into an homogenous whole.

During the summer offensive of 1942, individual operations carried out by Brandenburg groups secured bridges during the fighting south of Rostov and other bridges across the Byeloya river, en route to the Maikop oilfields.

The specialists of Brandenburg were used as assault infantry or on anti-partisan operations. Companies formed patrol boat detachments, whose task it was to prevent the landing of Soviet commandos on the shores of the Black Sea. Europe was not the only continent in which the Brandenburg units operated. Quite soon after the arrival of Rommel's Afrika Korps, 300 men under the command of Lieutenant von Koenen arrived to undertake deep penetrations of the British front, to attack lorried convoys, aerodromes and headquarters.

The history of von Koenen's group in Africa includes a long range mission of more than 2,000km to the Suez Canal to drop two intelligence officers, and British war diaries make frequent mention of 'Brandenburg' units. Rommel categorically refused to allow these detachments in Africa to disguise themselves in British uniform even though the British Army, according to a German report, had recruited German speaking Jews to carry out Brandenburg-type operations behind the German line while wearing German uniforms.

When in November 1942, the Allies landed in French North Africa a Brandenburg detachment took off from Bizerta and carried out a glider landed assault upon the railway bridge at Sid bou Bakir in Tunisia, and there were other operations to impede the Allied advance, one piece of work being against the Americans near Kasserine Pass on St Valentine's Day 1943. The defeat of the Axis armies in Africa was in sight and the Brandenburg specialists made their way back to Sicily and Italy where they regrouped and were soon in action again; in anti-partisan operations in the Balkans.

In an effort to expand the area of its operations and to subvert nations not wholly under Nazi control, Brandenburg officers took the unusual step of recruiting foreign prisoners of war, or disaffected natives of sensitive areas and then indoctrinating them. One such formation, raised during the winter of 1940/41, the Nightingale Battalion, so-called from the male voice choir which it boasted, was raised by 1st Regiment and made up of former West Ukrainian Polish soldiers who had been taken prisoner during the 1939 campaign. This battalion distinguished itself as part of the Brandenburg Regiment during the fighting around Lvov and, naively perhaps, declared itself to be the army of a free Ukraine. When the Germans refused to recognise the Ukraine as an independent state open mutiny broke out, and the battalion was disbanded.

Mutinies occurred in other 'Legions' made up of former Red Army men and in at least one case the German officers and NCOs were murdered. When the expansion came to divisional establishment one legion was attached to each regiment and 4th Regiment had under its command the so-called Indian Legion and a Persian company.

As has been explained in the first paragraphs of this section on Brandenburg the struggle for power between the *Abwehr* and the SD was won by the latter. Control then passed from Canaris and the *Ausland/Abwehr* to the SS and to Heinrich Himmler. The foreign legions, too, came into the SS sphere of influence. These legions then formed part of SS *Jagdverbände* (anti-partisan groups). The SS had little interest in the Brandenburg type of operation particularly since that formation had been an *Abwehr* unit. The specialist abilities of the regiments were completely ignored and the groups themselves put into infantry battles.

With no long-term prospects, isolated from the *Abwehr* and rejected by the SS, the pressure upon Brandenburg detachments to form a single command bore fruit and at the end of autumn 1942 a reorganisation took place. This resulted in an establishment along divisional lines with the cover name of 'Special Unit 800'. The reorganisation was completed by 1 November 1942, but the new division was not at that time outfitted with train or service units, for each of its detachments continued to be self-contained, carrying out operations in those areas of Europe which were their special responsibility.

As soon as it became possible to do so, battalions and other sub-units were withdrawn from the anti-partisan operations in which they were involved and posted to their regimental depot to be reorganised. This was no easy task and reformation proceeded only slowly but by 1 April 1943, all had been carried out and on that day Brandenburg Special

Purposes 800 Division was born. Some of the major divisional units were still in their depots, other groups were scattered across the length and breadth of Europe. Under such circumstances it is hardly surprising that a divisional loyalty was lacking and that it was to the regiment or, more usually, to the battalion and even the company that the men gave their allegiance.

Experiments connected with organisation were conducted to establish the perfectly balanced, all-arms combat unit, and in certain battalions specially designed battle groups were formed similar in composition, weapons and vehicles to the armoured personnel carrier companies of the panzer Grenadiers.

In addition to partisan warfare on the Soviet front, Brandenburg units were also posted to south-east Europe so that by the autumn of 1943, practically the whole division, though still fragmented, was operating in the Balkans. At the turn of the year some small elements were still on the Eastern Front, but the main was battling against rapidly growing partisan activity in Yugoslavia, Albania and northern Italy.

One action of 4th Regiment needs to be recounted if only to emphasise OKW's short-sighted attitude towards Brandenburg abilities. In an attempt to enlist support in the fight against Tito and his partisan bands the commander of 4th Jäger Regiment negotiated an understanding, almost an armistice, between his force and those troops led by the Serbian Chetnik hero, Draza Mihailovitch. The dialogue had progressed to a point where plans were being made to create a Montenegrin Legion within the establishment of 4th Regiment when on the direct order of OKW the discussions were broken off and the commanding officer threatened with a court martial for treating with the enemy. A possible chance to crush partisan activity in Yugoslavia was thrown away for the sake of protocol.

When in September 1943, Italy signed an armistice with the Allies, Brandenburg units seized the harbours of Albania and in Hungary held the Regent, Admiral Nikolaus von Horthy, prisoner until a government acceptable to Germany was formed.

On 13 September 1944, Brandenburg Division changed to become a panzer Grenadier unit, and with immediate effect was formed, together with the Panzer Grenadier Division Grossdeutschland, into a panzer corps. It was not until December 1944 that the main of the division could be brought together and one regiment, the 3rd, was in fact, never to be included within the divisional establishment. It proved impossible to withdraw it from its operational area in northern Italy and the men were posted to mountain units fighting in the Alpine area.

Even Brandenburg's panzer battalions did not go in to action as part of that division. One of them was posted to the Kurmark Panzer Division, born from a former sub-unit of Brandenburg and the second was destroyed in the fighting around Belgrade.

By the late summer of 1944, the satellite nations had begun to remove their support from Germany. Included among these was Romania and the loss of that country jeopardised the German line of communication to the west and opened a gap in the battle line. To counter the Soviet drive the German Army needed to establish a firm line east of the Danube. Brandenburg units were put in to fight for positions in eastern Yugoslavia to cover Belgrade, a vital communications centre, upon which the Red Army was advancing with top speed. Meanwhile immediate action needed to be taken to maintain communications to Romania. The Brandenburg parachute battalion was put in to hold the capital, Bucharest.

A small advance guard seized an airfield 14km north of Bucharest and during 24/25 August 1944, giant transport planes brought a force of over 2,000 men ready to march on Bucharest. During the night the political/military situation had deteriorated, for the balance had swung in favour of the Romanians. But the German Army in Romania was still a potent force and in an effort to save their capital city from the fierce fighting which might develop the Romanians offered the Brandenburg paratroop battalion safe conduct to the Yugoslavian border, and this was accepted by the officers of the battalion. By a ruse the senior commanders were removed from their men, Soviet armoured units came up, encircled the paratroops and declared the Red Army was not party to any safe conduct agreement. Leaderless and surrounded, the battalion surrendered thereby removing one of the last and most formidable blocks to the Soviet advance upon Belgrade.

There is much which could be written about the battle for Belgrade and the part which the Brandenburg units played in the defence of that city before they were removed and posted to the Grossdeutschland Panzer Corps. It must be sufficient to say here that the units fought well and when the order came to break through the ring of armour which the Soviet forces had flung around Belgrade, many detachments used the tricks and ruses of earlier days to escape the Soviet encirclement. Once through the Red lines the scattered sections were regrouped and ordered to drive in a Soviet bridgehead at Apatin, but a Red Army's break-out from that perimeter pre-empted the Brandenburg attack and the weak Brandenburg groups could do no more than slow the breakthrough. Continually delayed by having to fight such operations it was not until mid-December that the Brandenburg sub-units finally left the southern front to join the main body of the division in East Prussia.

Little remains to be reported of the division's activities on the Eastern Front which has not already been written in the preceding chapters and pages which cover the fighting operations in the USSR.

On the Western Front some units of Brandenburg seem to have been active almost until the final collapse of the Third Reich. In the late spring of 1945, a patrol of the Irish Guards intercepted a group of Germans and these proved to be Brandenburg men. Survivors of the Grossdeutschland Panzer Grenadier Division who had been absorbed into 15th Panzer Grenadier Division, on a basis of one Grossdeutschland Battalion to one of 15th Panzer Grenadier.

What the mission was which these men were to undertake went unrecorded in the Interrogation Report, but it seems unlikely that it could have been a spectacular one, nor one which could have at that late date, affected the outcome of the campaign in the west, in the way that a similar small group had affected the 1940 campaign at the Gennep bridge.

The original Brandenburg had grown from combat groups formed to protect factories, to battalions whose task it was to carry out missions of visibly strategic importance, like those in the early years of the war, to long range penetration patrols in Africa, by boat in Finland or by parachute drop in the distant reaches of the Asiatic Soviet Union, there to foment unrest, to destroy rail communications or to obstruct Allied plans.

And all this had been carried out without hope of recognition or anticipation of reward. A secret unit must retain its anonymity and those of its men who were awarded high decorations had no citation to indicate the daring deed which had caused them to be so honoured. Nor indeed could the identity or the role of the unit be given and it was not until later in the war when Brandenburg had given up its secret role and was a Panzer Grenadier Division that it was named for its part in the fighting on the Eastern Front. Unknown and almost unhonoured the men of the original Brandenburg served faithfully, forsaking the warrior's traditional and visible rewards for that abstract ideal which is embodied in the old Prussian soldiers' song which claims that 'he who joins the Prussian service has nothing any more which he can call his own – except duty'.

The Panzer Grenadier Division Kurmark

The military life of Panzer Grenadier Division Kurmark was short, hard and disastrous. Converted from a miscellany of Grossdeutschland remnants, mounted on bicycles and called an Army anti-tank unit it became *Kampfgruppe Langkeit,* whose assortment of armoured vehicles included tanks without guns and others with no turrets.

An operation during 26 and 27 January 1945 to break the Soviet armoured ring at Sternberg succeeded but, having brought out the encircled formations *Langkeit* Group itself had to be rescued and lost all its soft-skinned vehicles and heavy weapons.

During February the battle group was reformed as a counter-attack unit called the

General Langkeit, General officer commanding Kurmark Division.

Kurmark Division and took on charge sufficient, first-class armoured vehicles to raise its level of potency. It then moved to the Oder river to face the three Red Fronts which had halted there after the Soviet assaults ran out of impetus.

The last, major Soviet offensive opened on 16 April when behind a barrage fired by 22,000 guns, tens of thousands of infantrymen advanced in a night lit by artificial moonlight created by searchlights. During the second day of battle the divisions flanking Kurmark collapsed and a Soviet flood swept past and round it. A counter-attack in conjunction with scratch formations was ordered by 9th Army but was never launched. Soviet strength had grown too great to be halted by ad hoc groupings.

On 21 April the 9th Army, encircled by six Soviet armies, fell back to the river Spree. Its corps and divisions were isolated from each other, battling for their existence in the vast Colpin woods. Ahead of Kurmark lay a time in which the Panzer Grenadier Division was to be destroyed as a cohesive fighting force.

Division planned to break out of the Soviet encirclement at Halbe, and by cannibalisation and siphoning of fuel formed a panzer force to break the Soviet ring. Halbe seemed deserted as the armoured point unit entered to be followed by the remaining foot and vehicle columns. Then a hurricane of fire crashed down. There could be no manoeuvring here. Soviet armour ahead and their infantry in the houses prevented this, Soviet shells killed friend and foe indiscriminately and in Halbe that day the gutters did run red with blood. Fragments of bodies blown apart by the cannonade festooned fences and walls. The division fought for its life. Grenadiers stormed Soviet-held houses fighting without quarter, for who could take prisoners in such a situation? Waves of Soviet infantry pouring out of the Halbe woods recoiled as the Kurmark fire struck them. In the confusion division switched the direction of its breakout attempts; but in vain. Every escape route was under fire and not one yard of that bitter trek was lacking groups of huddled dead.

Kurmark as a formation died in the gloomy woods south-west of Frankfurt although isolated groups fought their way through the Soviet encirclement towards the Elbe where, rumour said, the Americans had a bridge which led into their zone. Of the whole of 9th Army less than 30,000 crossed over to the other side. The war was over.

Eight
Major Units which formed part of the Grossdeutschland Establishment: Führer Begleit and Führer Grenadier

Hollywood films and the more sensational type of fiction have led us to believe that during the war the protection of Adolf Hitler depended completely and solely upon the SS. This belief is erroneous. From the time that an Army unit was first raised to guard the German Chancellor in 1938 until July 1944, when the bomb plot gave Hitler cause to doubt the Army's loyalty, the duties at his tactical headquarters were carried out by a unit which had had its beginnings in the Wach Regiment Berlin; the predecessor of the Grossdeutschland units.

By 1938 the Führer had need to move outside the former borders of Germany and to protect him on these excursions a unit at constant readiness, code named *Führer Reise* (Leader Journey), was formed during 1938. It was made up of motorised platoons from two companies of the Wach Regiment Berlin and command of this new formation was given to Colonel, later Field-Marshal, Rommel.

Men for the Führer unit were drawn first from the Wach Regiment then from the Grossdeutschland Regiment and the group, which had escorted Hitler during the Polish campaign, then formed the cadre around which a Führer Begleit Battalion was formed and to which colours were presented during October 1939.

The escort detachment accompanied Hitler to France during the fighting in the west in 1940 and on 22 June of that year three trumpeters of No. 1 Company of the Führer Begleit Battalion blew the formal 'cease fire' at 20.00hr to mark the end of hostilities.

During June 1941, Hitler moved to Rastenburg and into the headquarters which have become familiar as the *Wolfsschaare* and in which the unsuccessful assassination was attempted on 20 July 1944.

A unit which is selected to guard a national leader cannot suffer from the stigma of being thought to be non-combatant and yet the task of protecting the leader has to be its paramount duty. The German solution to this problem was to form a battlegroup – Kampfgruppe Nehring – and to rotate men to and from this to gain front line experience. The original intention to limit this period to three months duration in the northern part of the line could not be maintained. The crisis which developed during that first winter in the USSR kept the Kampfgruppe in the line, for often it was the only well-equipped reserve which could be put in at critical points. To meet the new demands which were then made upon it the establishment was increased to include a panzer company, an anti-tank, a motorcycle, a reconnaissance and a flak platoon as well as signals, medical and workshop detachments.

During its period in the line, Battle Group Nehring was split up among nearby divisions and this unfortunate destruction of the unit's potential was one with which all Grossdeutschland units were to become familiar during the latter stages of the war. Kampfgruppe Nehring was never able to fight as a single unit under its own commander during its first operation and being on detached duty, separated from its parent unit, suffered badly in respect of rations, clothing and accommodation as well as being given the most difficult military tasks to perform. The results were inevitable and the panzer company, taken here as just one example, had lost all its Panzer I vehicles by the time it was withdrawn from the line at the end of March 1942.

During the Soviet winter offensive of '42/43 another crisis developed and once again battle groups from the Führer Begleit Battalion were called for to seal gaps in the line. The great Soviet offensive had torn away the satellite armies and had smashed through and German Army. A miscellany of units was rushed in to seal off the open gap and among these was a rifle company, a heavy weapons company and a panzer company of the Führer Begleit Battle Group.

In comparison with the numbers which were needed this small combat command may have seemed puny, but this was a battle group made up of first-class fighting men, magnificently equipped and well armed with anti-tank weapons. The group then served in the line from the end of February until being returned to the battalion at Rastenburg in April.

During the fighting in which Grossdeutschland Division was engaged around Kharkov during 1943, a new crisis demanded that practically the whole Führer Begleit Battalion be committed leaving only a small guard detachment on duty at the Führer's headquarters. It had already become obvious that there needed to be a purely guard/security formation as well as a combat unit within the battalion's establishment. Out of the Führer Begleit Battalion a Führer Grenadier Battalion was born during April

1943 and as a recognition of the ability of the Führer Begleit it was raised to the status of a panzer Grenadier unit during June 1943.

At the end of that year the Soviets opened their third, great winter offensive and by the second week of January 1944 their blows against Army Group North had had such success that Führer HQ had to order a strong Begleit Battle Group to reinforce the Narva front.

From 9 February, the first day of its new action, until its withdrawal from the line on 18 May, the battle group fought hard and well. Not only had it been required to protect the main highway and to halt the onrushing Soviet offensive, but it had also had to guard the sea flank against Soviet landings.

Upon their return to Fighter HQ and as a result of the experience which had been gained during these missions a suggestion was made, and quickly taken up, that there should be a regiment raised to be on permanent standby: a Führer's fire brigade, ready to be put in wherever there was a critical situation. The Führer Begleit Battalion was then expanded to regimental strength during May 1944, the men being obtained from the Panzer Grenadier Replacement Brigade Grossdeutschland.

By the end of June 1944, the serious shortage of infantry required that new techniques be adopted to save manpower without reducing the fire power of front line formations and the new weapons meant that one man would have the fire-power that five men had had at the outbreak of war, but it was important to use these new powers in the most efficient way. German success in forming Kampfgruppen posed the problem for military planners which was the correct balance of all arms and new types of unit known as small panzer brigades were formed. In addition to a headquarters staff their composition included a panzer battalion, an armoured personnel carrier battalion, a panzer Grenadier battalion as well as a number of companies, including reconnaissance engineers, anti-tank, signals SP flak, and infantry gun on SP mountings.

One of the first of these small panzer brigades to be established was the Führer Grenadier Brigade while its parent formation was now known, unofficially, as the Führer Begleit Regiment.

A fresh critical situation on the northern sector of the Eastern Front required that a battle group be sent out from the Führer Begleit to raise the siege of Vilna and to hold that place. It seemed as if the correct combination of men, arms and equipment had been truly established. The order then came that the regiment had been raised to become Führer Begleit Brigade and that it, too should be modelled on the lines of the small panzer brigade.

Then came a new proposal. It was suggested that from divisions with excellent combat records a brigade strength battle group would be taken to form a cadre around which a new elite division could be created. The end result of this was not to produce two elite divisions but two mediocre formations. The officers of the Führer units were wiser than most regimental officers and took to posting away key men for short courses whenever there was a risk that these might be taken from their own units.

During the latter weeks of September 1944, the Führer Grenadier Brigade was posted to East Prussia and OKH Reserve. It was not to remain long uncommitted to battle for Stavka was determined to clear its northern battle flank by seizing East Prussia and brought together five Red Armies totalling some forty infantry divisions backed with adequate armoured and artillery force. Facing this massive build-up there was the 4th German Army, under strength, but experienced and still capable. The 4th Army defending East Prussia, that is to say a battle line 350km in length, could muster only seven battle tested infantry divisions, six of the newly raised Volksgrenadier divisions, some police divisions and a couple of cavalry brigades. In the whole of 4th Army area there were no mobile reserves available.

The attack by 3rd Byelo-Russian Front came in during 16 October on a narrow sector and was accompanied by armour and bombardments by land and air on an unprecedented scale. There was no subtlety in the Soviet assault, merely a frontal attack. Along 4th Army front the Red Army made penetrations and the Guards assault on the following day carried the advance forward to Gumbinnen. 4th Army began to disintegrate.

Reinforcements were needed and speed was all important. Immediately available was the Führer Grenadier Brigade from OKH Reserve and a further two elite divisions, all of whom were ordered to take up position west and north-west of Goldap. By the 20th the new units were under command of 4th Army and in position ready to trap and encircle the Soviet forces.

The task of the Führer Grenadier Brigade in this move was to strike northwards into the flank and to excise the Red armour spearhead. At dawn on the morning of 21 October the Führer Grenadier Brigade moved out pushing forward until the Panzer Grenadier Battalion bumped the enemy at noon. General fighting then broke out. By last light the Führer Grenadier Brigade was positioned around Draken having expelled the Soviets and driven them back.

Then Fusilier Battalion took up the assault which moved forward across the Rominte river, pushing on until it was halted by squadrons of T.34s and KVs. The battalion was still not on its objective, but without armour no forward movement could be made and by last light the outcome had still not been decided. The battalion comaunder wirelessed for Panthers to clear the Red armour from the road ahead.

During the advance of the Führer Grenadier Brigade the Soviet command aware of the threat of encirclement re-grouped their forces for a counter-stroke. This pre-emptive blow came in at dawn on the 22nd and the panzer battalion could now no longer be sent forward to support the Fusiliers for it was drawn into battle against a mass of Soviet tanks protected by a deep pak front. Under cover of this sudden strike the Soviet Command withdrew the infantry and armour from the salient towards the only avenue of escape; the Rominte bridge which the Führer Grenadier Fusilier Battalion now dominated.

Against the thin Fusilier line the Soviets flung their armour and infantry. When the Panthers did hold off the T.34s then wave after wave of Red Army infantry charged across the open fields and engaged in hand to hand fighting with the Fusiliers. By the end of the day thirty Soviet tanks lay broken and smashed.

The initial encirclement strengthened by the other divisions of 4th Army, compressed the Soviets into a very small area and they made frenzied efforts to escape from the encirclement. Their struggles brought crises to the men of the Panzer Grenadier Battalion during the afternoon of 22 October when in an effort to force the Grenadiers from their positions, Stavka sent in squadrons of aircraft and massed armour behind which there advanced lines of troops from a Guards infantry division. Waves of these elite troops swept across the forward outposts of the Führer Grenadier Brigade and turned the battalions' position on both flanks.

Even the arrival of a Panther tank into this bitter little fight could not conceal the fact that the situation for the panzer Grenadiers had deteriorated and that only withdrawal could save the unit from extinction. A link-up on 27 October with other divisions released the Führer Grenadier Brigade into reserve. Soon it was brought forward again in an offensive to re-capture Goldap in collaboration with 5th Panzer and 50th Infantry Divisions. On 2/3 November the Panzer Grenadier Battalion supporting 5th Panzer gained all the given objectives, but the Soviets had anticipated the assault by the 50th Division and the Fusilier Battalion was smashed and shot to pieces. Shaking off its losses the brigade pressed on with the attack until Goldap was recaptured.

The Führer Grenadier Brigade went into reserve on 30 November and was brought up to the establishment of a reinforced panzer brigade while Führer Begleit Brigade was converted to become a panzer brigade.

The Führer Units in the battle for the Ardennes, December 1944-January 1945

Within a few weeks of the Führer Brigades leaving the line on the Eastern Front they were back in action again, this time fighting against the Western Allies in Belgium. This was an attack aimed at seizing the port of Antwerp, by an advance through the Ardennes and across the Meuse. In the event, things did not quite work out according to the Führer's plan. The timetable for the operation could not be kept and towns which should have been captured within hours of the opening of the offensive were defended tenaciously by their American infantry and tank Corps garrisons.

By 18 December, that is within forty-eight hours of the opening of the assault, it was dear that 1st SS Panzer Division Leibstandarte SS Adolf Hitler could not break out of the river valleys in which it was trapped and that the task of bringing the attack forward had passed to 5th Panzer Army.

To add impetus to this the Führer Brigade was ordered forward on the 16th, but blocked roads had halted it and the tail-back extended for nearly 60km into Germany. The main of the brigade grouped itself east of St Vith where the Americans laid down barrages which halted the brigade's first sally. It regrouped and swung out again but was brought up short by a pak front. While the brigade was halted a Volksgrenadier Division occupied the road which had been reserved for the Führer Begleit vehicles so that the commanding officer found his line of march blocked by the chiefly horse-drawn vehicles The orders to the Brigade Commander had been clear – do not become embroiled in fighting to gain St Vith – but with his road forward choked the Commander calculated that a quick thrust might yet seize the town and allow his columns to cover the ground to the river by a more direct route. The Panzer Grenadiers went in and were beaten back by the Americans. The columns swung around the town but deep mud and heavy artillery fire destroyed the symmetry of the assault.

An officers' patrol from the Führer Begleit Brigade went out to attack the US artillery whose fire was impeding the advance, but the patrol was itself attacked and destroyed. The end of the day brought only the satisfaction of knowing that now St Vith was cut off from the main body of the US Army.

During the 19th, the first elements of Führer Grenadier Brigade took post south on the left flank of 5th Panzer Army, to protect this from the attacks which the regrouped and aggressive American units were now making against the German salient. By now, those overcast skies which the Führer had promised would ground the Allied air force, had lifted and the German vehicle columns were exposed and visible to the fighter-bombers of the RAF and the USAAF which swooped down upon them. On the southern side of the salient the Führer Grenadier Brigade had been unable to make ground and was forced on to the defensive along the line of the river Sauer, beating back US attempts to establish bridgeheads across that waterway. The fighting swayed to and fro, as the Führer Grenadier battled to establish a stable front and the Americans tried to force 5th Panzer Army back and to reach Bastogne. The Allied counter-attacks were now well co-ordinated with pressure exerted from the south and south-west by the 3rd Army and from the north and north-west by the British 30 Corps, the 30th US Division and 7th US Armoured Division. American counter-attacks overran 3rd Battalion of Führer Begleit and it lost men continually until the panzer and the SPs roared forward to smash the Allied tank thrust destroying twenty tanks in short order. The panzer counter-attack brought the German line forward and the brigade advanced crushing all opposition. At dawn on 24 December contact was made with elements of 6th SS Panzer Army under whose command the Führer Begleit now passed. On 26th the brigade was taken out of the line and put in with an SS assault to cast a ring around Bastogne. 1st Battalion was not able to disengage until the onset of darkness and even then had to endure severe barrages as it foot-marched to its new combat area.

Both Führer Brigades were suffering such losses that it could only be a question of time before they ceased to be effective as fighting formations. In the Grenadier Brigade average company strengths were now only thirty men and within the whole brigade only twenty-five armoured fighting vehicles or SPs could still be considered as fit for action. Despite their weakness both brigades strove desperately to reach the Meuse. The situation was very confused. To the west of Bastogne Führer Begleit formed part of the northern arm of a pair of pincers which were trying to cut off the town. The southern pincer arm contained the Führer Grenadier Brigade battling furiously to hold open the road from Harlange to Donkholtz.

Reconnaissance carried out by the Grenadier Brigade showed that 3rd US Army had forced the line of the Sauer river presenting the threat that if they linked with the forces still inside Bastogne then the left wing of 5th Panzer Army might be cut off from the main body.

The military initiative had swung to the Allies but both brigades still continued their by now pointless assaults. In and around Chenogne one assault died on the open slopes when the last survivors realised that alone and unsupported they could achieve nothing.

SS Corps during 29 December ordered that the attack be resumed during the 30th and from every sub-unit of the Begleit Brigade men were drawn to form infantry detachments so that the order could be complied with. As the attack began to roll at 07.30hr on the morning of the 30th the appearance of US tank columns on the road indicated that the Begleit assault had pre-empted the Americans and that both attacks would collide. The panzer and the armoured personnel vehicles swung out and into hull down positions waiting until the US combat machines had come within range. By the end of the day thirty American armoured fighting vehicles lay smashed for a loss of four of the Führer Begleit machines.

Faced with American probes all along the front, SPs and other panzer vehicles were rushed from one threatened point to another. Grenadiers fought with *Panzerfaust* as day succeeded day with bitter fighting for the ruins of houses along the battle line. Down the southern flank where the Führer Grenadier Brigade held post the fighting had been just as bitter as that on the northern shoulder where the Führer Begleit was in position.

Villages lost to the Grenadier Brigade were ordered to be recaptured and immediate counter-attacks carried out in the face of barrages of artillery and fighter-bombers reduced the companies to vanishing point. The small town of Dahl had been taken from a Volksgrenadier unit and orders came to the panzer Grenadiers of the Führer Grenadier Brigade that it had to be retaken. The depleted battalion went in at dawn wading through the thigh deep snow, shivering in their soaked uniforms as they advanced through the bitter icy morning. The attack could not be described as having been made with a swing but the forward movement was always maintained and the first houses were stormed and taken. Then the assault groups came under fire from the US infantry and the first groups of Grenadiers were swept away. The US troops moved into their own counter-attack and the Grenadiers were flung out of Dahl and down the slopes of the hill up which they had waded only hours before. Of all the men who had taken part in the assault less than eighty reached regimental tactical headquarters.

Other elements of the brigade were acting as 'stiffeners' to hold the crumbling front but it was clear that the Führer Grenadier Brigade was now ineffective as a fighting force and it was withdrawn from the line on 16 January.

The German forces retired from the bulge and the pace of the withdrawal accelerated as orders came to make for Wiompont where there was a bridge, one of the few which had not been blown. The road back presented the same scenes of confusion as had the roads forward when the offensive had opened. Shortage of fuel meant that vehicles with petrol were towing those whose tanks were dry and along the roads were abandoned lorries, guns and armoured vehicles. The battle of the Ardennes was nearly over. For the Germans in the west this was the only time since D-Day, 6 June, that they had held the overall initiative and now this short-lived superiority had been wrested from them. Their last hope had died.

The Führer Begleit too was withdrawn from the line during the night of 11/12 January, but was back again on 14th to carry out an attack to hold off the pursuing Americans. By now the intense cold, the snow, the lack of food and the exposure were taking their toll; bronchitis and respiratory illnesses of all sorts as well as frostbite, were thinning the ranks of those who had survived the battles.

The step by step fighting withdrawal continued with both Führer Brigades fighting side by side to cover the evacuation of the main body. The fighting retreat ended and on 25 January came the news that both brigades were to be expanded to divisional strength. The new units to reinforce and to bring them up to strength were ready and waiting. The Führer's fire brigade which had once been a battalion strong had now grown in size to become two divisions fully equipped with lavish establishments and armed with the most modern combat equipment.

By the middle of January 1945 the great Soviet winter offensive was pushing northwards and westwards towards Kustrin to gain bridgeheads across the river Oder at that place.

At this stage of the war there could be no question of the German Army undertaking any sort of major offensive against the Soviet mass. Local attacks with limited objectives were all that could be mounted and for one rash enterprise troops had been assembled by scraping together every possible soldier and this mass was directed to strike at the rear of the Soviet salient which was pushing towards Kustrin. To act in the role of 'firemen' Führer Begleit and Führer Grenadier Brigades were withdrawn from the west and were hurried eastwards.

The role which Hitler proposed for the two new Führer Divisions was to have them outside a formal Corps, Army or Army Group allegiance, so that they were always available to be thrown into counter-attacks. It was to enable them to carry out this independent role that neither Führer unit was included within the establishment of Grossdeutschland Corps although they had had their genesis in that unit.

During February both divisions began to arrive in eastern Germany and were sent in to halt the Soviet thrust for Stettin. Their immediate task was to prevent the cutting of a railway supply line which nourished 3rd Panzer Army and they struck southwards to the Netz river, there to take in flank and to destroy the Red forces which had reached the Oder. Hitler's intention was to use Army Group Vistula's right wing which lay along the Oder and its left wing east of Arnswalde, to encircle the Soviets and, thereby, to achieve in Pomerania an important – in his belief a decisive – victory.

This was an operation accorded the highest priority. Such was its urgency and so great the Soviet pressure against the weak German line that the armoured fighting vehicles of the Führer Begleit SP Company roared straight from the detraining point into the attack. Despite initial successes the Red infantry struck back in counter-attacks and the battle line swayed to and fro as German attack was followed by a Soviet counter-thrust. During day and even by night Soviet pressure was maintained and the dark February skies were lit up by the sudden flames from *Panzerfaust* and *Panzerschreck* as the Grenadiers fought the T.34s and KVs at close range in the vast forests of Pomerania or stalked them across the low and rolling hills.

Strong Soviet pressure forced the German Command to regroup its forces into two strong battle groups and thereby the expressed intention to keep the Führer Divisions as elite counter-attack units disappeared when Führer Begleit was absorbed into one of these groups. The division had lost its role almost within weeks of being formed.

A plan worked out by the battle group commanders to resume the attack and to strike for the Oder during the night of 12/13 February failed. The offensive upon which Hitler had placed such high hopes had been bogged down. On 16 February the Führer Grenadier Division was brought forward to support the flagging assault but the Soviet Command regrouped its forces and counter-attacked in such strength that by the afternoon of 18 February it was clear to the German commanders that to continue with the offensive would result in the destruction of the Führer Divisions. The German battle line receded

Men of the Grossdeutschland with a Panzerschreck.

and the Divisions pulled back in good order to their start lines.

Another crisis brought them to attack the town of Lauban, a junction on the supply route to Breslau. The Army Commander's ambitious plan was for a double encirclement around the town and for this task he assembled the two Führer, the 17th Panzer and the 8th Panzer Divisions. None of these was, however, a fresh unit filled with men and up to establishment in vehicles, but the remnant of a division – men tired and battle weary with tanks that were short of fuel, of spares and of maintenance.

The assault opened during the night of 1/2 March and at first all four columns of divisions made progress, but then they were enmeshed in heavily wooded areas which slowed the advance and allowed the Soviets to set up pak fronts on every avenue of approach. The Führer Grenadier Division did manage to force a bridgehead across the river Queis but this was driven in by Soviet counter-attacks.

The slow advance formed a salient under fire from three sides as the German units struggled forward. Behind the leading units the salient walls were held by a thin line of Grenadiers against which Soviet tanks battalions were flung regardless of loss until eventually a breakthrough was made. It was clear that the offensive could not succeed.

However slow the German advance may have been it was still powerful enough to cause deep concern to the Soviet Command and they evacuated Lauban rather than have their troops trapped there. Then, true to their training, they counter-attacked and forced back Führer Begleit with heavy loss.

The German offensive was dying, but the Army commander called for one last effort and this, brought forward by the determined Grenadiers, almost closed the pincer jaws around the now almost deserted town. The number of prisoners taken was small and the achievements minimal when compared to the losses which the Führer Divisions had suffered.

The final battles of the Führer Begleit Division

From the middle week of March the German front on the Oder at last hardened and halted the Red Army's advance. The Soviet main effort was then taken up by 4th Ukrainian Front in whose sector less ground had been gained due to the determined defence of 1st Panzer Army.

This Red Front now struck deep in a south-westerly drive along the line Troppau/Jagendorf encountering little serious resistance once it had overrun the forward line. This was, by that stage of the war, not unusual for there were now no fresh and uncommitted reserves which could be put in. The policy of the Supreme Commander in his underground bunker in Berlin was to switch his fire brigade units from one threatened sector to another and these frenzied moves were made without regard to the fact that the fighting strength of such units was absent from the line. This unplanned movement of elite, major groupings up and down the length of the eastern battle front denuded the line and directly aided the Red advance.

One unit posted during this critical period was the Führer Begleit Division and it was taken by train from Lauban and sent to Jagendorf.

The situation facing the division upon its arrival at Jagendorf was one familiar to the old soldier, veterans of the Eastern Front, but was bewildering to those volunteer recruits who had come fresh to war. There was no cohesive defence, no idea of the enemy's location, the direction of weight of his thrust nor the number of his host. There were few liaison officers to guide the unit into those positions from which it would be able to strike with maximum effect at the onthrusting Soviet forces; no experienced voices to advise on good defensive positions or lines of assault. If the term fog of war had any reality then it was thickest there, on the Jagendorf sector and the men pitched into battle as fast as they arrived at their rail destination felt that they were a forlorn hope.

Early in the morning of 23 March, Führer Begleit detrained and the division's officers regrouped their units, established them in hastily dug positions, gained touch with neighbouring units and prepared their men to meet the imminent Soviet thrust.

The first shells of the Soviet artillery fell during 25 March; the assault could not now be far off. Battle group patrols told of the approach of a small column of Red armour and infantry driving south-westwards.

Soviet probing attacks came in now all along the line looking for weak spots in the German defences and one particularly savage blow on 26 March began an ever increasing series of assaults to drive back the Panzer Grenadiers and to force them from a chain of heights from which they dominated the battle area. To hold down the men of the Führer Division, the Soviet Air Force brought into the battle its fighter-bomber aircraft, but in vain. The T.34s and the KVs escorted the brown clad infantry across the open fields and meadows sparkling in the late March sunshine. One attack after the other was flung back; dying in the fierce defensive fire which was poured down upon the long lines of Soviet infantry. During one day's fighting no fewer than thirty Soviet armoured fighting vehicles were destroyed or set on fire; the infantry dead were never counted. The German line held even though wastage through casualties was no longer being replaced and the battle line was becoming too weak to maintain such a dogged defence.

Where it was necessary, local counter-attacks were put in to recapture some tactically important piece of ground but Soviet pressure had become too great and slowly the Grenadiers were forced back from the high ground which they had defended for nearly a week against overwhelming odds. Small groups of men, the survivors of companies or platoons overrun and blown apart by the T.34s regrouped to hold one line after the other, but each of these was forced back by some new assault.

On the final day of March a divisional effort was made to cut off another Soviet spearhead filtering through the German lines. At dawn the last panzer vehicles of the Führer Begleit Panzer Regiment led into the attack the infantry survivors of the Panzer Grenadier Regiments, supported by the remaining SPs and the divisional artillery. The attack roared through a curtain of fire and struck deep into the Soviet flank halting the westward drive. The Soviet spearhead recoiled, regrouped and then struck forward but was driven back each time. The battle which swayed around the Prussian villages was of an intensity and of a bitterness that even four years of war had not matched. For many men this was their home and hearth for which they were fighting and the loss of every foot of German soil meant its surrender to the enemy. Each Soviet thrust was met by a counter-blow and the loss of a single house brought forward a Grenadier assault to recover it. Fighting at such an intense pace brought such heavy losses that during the dark of the nights the last reinforcements, the specialists of assault companies, had to be brought forward to thicken the weakening line.

The line which was now kept by isolated small groups, sometimes by only two men and a machine-gun or a *Panzerfaust,* held until the unit was relieved on 3 April, and the exhausted Grenadiers moved back from a battlefield upon which lay 231 Soviet tanks.

On 16 April the Soviet assault which was to end the war in Europe opened along the Lausnitze/Neisse line. Despite the bitter defence, Soviet armour poured through the gaps and in the area in which the Führer Begleit Division lay the Soviet thrusts penetrated as far as the divisional rest area.

The defence then put up by Führer Begleit forced the Red tankmen to swing round the division and Soviet spearheads had in fact reached past the divisional sector. The Eastern Front was crumbling but still at certain points local assaults went in and the division was ordered to stand fast and act as a wall defending an SS assault. Führer Begleit held the line but the SS Corps attack was crushed and it died in the face of massed armour and pak fronts. The Führer Begleit was once again cut off from the German line and it had to fight its way through Soviet-held territory to reach the safety of its own lines.

The events during the night of 20/21 April 1945 are important in the story of the Führer Begleit for during those hours the last collective and centrally organised attack which the division made during the Second World War was undertaken. This was a death or glory mission, of that there could be no doubt. Unserviceable vehicles were destroyed; most of the panzers, lacking fuel, were blown up. Two battle groups of men were formed; these were large bodies for, by now, scattered groups of soldiers from other formations joined the division hoping to gain the security and protection of a major unit or determined to join an organised body and to fight the Soviet invaders to the last.

A commanders' conference decided that the Führer Begleit armour would lead the break-out. All the wounded would be taken with the main body.

During the night the Soviets had not been idle and had strengthened the ring which they had cast around the division. When the first reconnaissances were made during 22 April, the westward road to Neu Petershain was found to be blocked in force. A change of direction was ordered to escape through the only remaining gap. The move southwards began and none who survived it ever forgot it. This was nothing less than a shooting gallery for the Soviet infantry and armour. The German force had to retreat across completely open country; from west and from east the Soviet machine-guns and artillery fired at point blank range as the columns raced across the open fields. The German losses were enormous. Whole groups of men were mown down by the Soviet machine-guns and even in death they were not left in peace, for artillery salvoes bursting among the bodies flung these through the air, blew them to pieces and reduced them to bloodied fragments of flesh. Along the whole corridor of death, tanks lay burning – Soviet as well as German – for though this may have been a withdrawal it was not a rout and the panzers took the opportunity to strike back blowing apart the T.34s with the final rounds in their ammunition lockers. Nor were the infantrymen idle and they battered to death with entrenching tools the crews of Soviet machine-gun posts which they overran in their burst for freedom.

The Führer Begleit Division died on the ghastly meadows of New Petershain and of all the mass which had set out to break through, less than 400 succeeded in crossing the Elbe river on barrels or any piece of flotsam and reporting themselves to the headquarters of the Grossdeutschland Panzer Corps in Dresden. Throughout the succeeding days the Führer Begleit group organised as a small battle group fought on against the overwhelming Soviet pressure and even as late as 6 May, part of that battle group, led by the divisional commander, was still in action near Dresden before being forced during that day across the Erzgebirge, where it surrendered to the Soviets when the war ended on 7 May.

The final battles of the Führer Grenadier Division

While the Führer Begleit Division had been fighting the Soviet assaults along the Oder line and deep inside Saxony the Führer Grenadier unit had had its own battles and had met its own fate.

Towards the end of March 1945, orders came to despatch the Führer Grenadier Brigade with all possible speed to Vienna, there to counter the Red offensive which was menacing the capital city.

As early as 6 April the 4th and 6th Red Guards Armies had opened the assault upon Vienna and by the same evening had won a small foothold in its suburbs.

The subsequent battle for the city was confusing, not least for the men of the Führer Grenadier Division for there were within the city a number of Austrians who now saw their chance to liberate their country from the Germans and who guided Red Army units past road blocks which had been set up. The Führer Grenadier was ordered to attack towards Klosterneuburg against the forces of 6th Guards Armoured Army which were striking down from the north of the Vienna woods. En route to their new mission the vehicle columns of the Führer Grenadier Division were surprised by the appearance in the centre of the city of Red Army tank columns and street fighting broke out as the Grenadiers sought to drive the Red Guards back from the area of the western railway station.

On 7 April the Red Army cut off Vienna. Fierce fighting took place as the SS troops of 1st Panzer Corps and the men of the Führer Grenadier Division beat back the assaults, but the unequal struggle could not last long and on 8 April the commander of Army Group South ordered the evacuation of the city. The task of Führer Grenadier was now to break through the Soviet armour ring by striking across the Danube and there to collaborate with the remnants of 9th Panzer Division in holding all Soviet advances on the northern bank of the river.

The last evacuations from Vienna took place during the night of 12 April and the slow withdrawal of the remnants of Army Group South from the Soviet pincer jaws continued until by 26 April a defensive line was reached and held until 1 May, against all the furious assaults of 49th Guards Infantry Division. During that day information was received at Army Group Headquarters of an armistice which was to be signed on the following day. The war was in its last stages and it was now imperative that the men of Army Group South be saved from Soviet imprisonment. The Army Group Commander ordered his forces to disengage from the Soviets and to make for the American lines where they were to surrender.

A rearguard was needed to hold the line while the remainder of the Army Group's divisions and Corps escaped. The choice fell upon the remnants of the Führer Grenadier Division who took up a line in and around Krems and held it until the order came to join the general withdrawal. The unit passed as an organised body through the streams of refugees, fragmenting battalions, foreign workers and the chaos of a retreating Army until it reached Trakwein on 9 May where it surrendered to the US forces.

There remained one final twist to the story of the Führer Grenadier Division. One night, shortly after the surrender, the American guards melted quietly into the night and when dawn came there were new sentries – men of the Red Army. Ahead of all the men of the Führer Grenadier Division now lay years of imprisonment and for many death in the vast territory of the Soviet Union.

Appendix 1
The Uniform for the Infantry Regiment Grossdeutschland

The especially designed uniform jacket proposed for the Infantry Regiment Grossdeutschland was modelled on the normal field grey army uniform tunic but was piped in white Waffenfarbe down the front over lap of the tunic, down the front of and around the collar base, on the upper edges of the cuffs and around the cuff-patterns as well as on the edging to the jacket tails at the rear. Buttons were in matt finish white metal.

The jacket had two specially notable features in that the collar-patches and cuff-patterns were of a design completely different to any other German Army uniform introduced during the Third Reich period. These features were deliberately chosen for this 'new' formation in order to convey a sense of continuing tradition with the Imperial German Army of 1914. Elite regiments of all old Imperial States wore *Doppelitzen,* an elongated, lace collar patch and 'French cuffs' were a feature of Imperial German Army uniform worn only by the Garde Schützen Bataillon and the 2 Garde MG Abteilung. The adoption of this particular style of collar patch and cuff pattern was a deliberate attempt to identify Grossdeutschland with the traditions of the old Imperial Army.

The collar patches were of a special design 13cm long in silver embroidery and worked directly on to the dark blue-green collar and, unlike normal infantry parade collar patches, were without any white Waffenfarbe underlay cloth. On both cuffs of this special tunic were worn French cuff patterns of dark blue-green backing cloth. They were piped round the edge with white Waffenfarbe piping and on each cuff pattern there were three separate silver embroidered cuff-patches each with a matt finished white metal button without any white Waffenfarbe underlay. Shoulder straps worn on the tunic carried the entwined Grossdeutschland shoulder strap monogram in white. The straps themselves were of dark blue-green material piped white.

On the lower right arm, 1cm above the top edge of the French cuff, was worn the newly issued Grossdeutschland cuff title, 3.2cm wide with Gothic style lettering in fine silver aluminium thread machine embroidered on to a dark green band. The national emblem backed with dark blue-green material was worn on the right breast.

The NCO pattern uniform differed from the one described above in three points. Rank braiding 0.9cm wide was worn around the upper edges to the Swedish cuffs, behind the French cuff facing patterns. This rank braiding was also displayed around the upper edge to, and down the front of, the collar, necessitating the use of only a single bar of patch *litzen* instead of the double lace braiding worn by other ranks and officers. The Grossdeutschland monogram shoulder straps displayed the NCO's rank.

Due to the outbreak of the war this jacket was never issued.

Greatcoat

Although similar in style and colour to the normal pattern worn throughout the German Army in peacetime by all ranks (other than by generals), this greatcoat had a collar much larger than normal with deep collar points and faced with the universal dark blue-green material. It was edged with white piping which was also carried around the upper edges to the deep turn-back cuffs.

Above the turn-back cuff of the right sleeve was worn the silver-on-green cuff-title Grossdeutschland. All other details were the same as the standard pattern German Army greatcoat.

Cuff Titles

On 27 June 1939 all ranks of the Infantry Regiment Grossdeutschland were authorised to wear as the special distinction a cuff band on their lower right sleeve. These had not been issued by the outbreak of war and were not, in fact, on general issue until 24 August 1940.

Dress Regulations stated that the band was to be of green cloth but at the instigation of the regimental commander the background colour was changed from green to black. Cuff bands of this pattern, black with silver aluminium thread, were issued both to the Grossdeutschland Regiment and to the Führer Begleit Battalion on 7 October 1940.

During the war there were to be four changes to this original pattern of cuff band. The original black and earlier green bands had had the unit name woven in Gothic letters. The subsequent three patterns had the inscription changed to standard German script but then there was a reversion to the original letter style and to Gothic characters. In every case, however, the cuff band had a top and bottom line of aluminium thread.

All units which emerged from the original Grossdeutschland detachments were entitled to wear the Grossdeutschland cuff title and this concession was granted to the Panzer Division Kurmark, which was not raised until January 1945. In the case of those units of the Grossdeutschland organisation which had their own identifying name, for example *Führerhauptquartier*, then the cuff title with that name was usually the only one worn. There were, however, cases where some men wore two cuff bands; one on each sleeve.

Shoulder Straps

Shoulder straps and epaulettes for the Wach Regiment Berlin carried an initial W in white woven cloth for other ranks and in white metal for officers. When the regiment was renamed and became Grossdeutschland then the monogram Grossdeutschland in entwined capitals was carried and, with the expansion of the unit to divisional status, a numeral '1' or '2' was worn below the monogram to show regimental allegiance.

The shoulder straps and epaulettes of men of the Infantry Regiment Grossdeutschland were piped in white cloth to show that the wearer's arm of service was the infantry and that colour was retained even when the 1st Regiment was renamed as a Grenadier Regiment during 1940.

Upon the raising of the former Infantry Regiment to divisional status during 1942, a second regoment of foot was raised. This was titled Fusilier to distinguish it from the Grenadier Regiment and as a further distinction the arm of service colour worn piped round the shoulder straps was red.

When, during the last months of the Second World War, the Panzer Corps Grossdeutschland was formed, a third Regiment – a corps infantry formation – needed to be raised.

As an alternative from the standard arm of service colouring the Panzer Reconnaissance Battalion Grossdeutschland wore the golden/yellow cavalry colour on their shoulder straps and epaulettes.

Other Markings

Towards the end of 1939, the Grossdeutschland regimental commander decided that the vehicles of his unit would carry a distinctive emblem and that this emblem would be a white, German-pattern steel helmet within a frame. The various shapes of frame distinguished the various battalions of the regiment. 1st Battalion had a square, 2nd Battalion a circle, the 3rd Battalion a triangle and the 4th Battalion a diamond shape. Colours were used to distinguish the various companies within each battalion.

With the expansion of the regiment to become a division this system fell into disuse and unit identification changed to an unframed single white steel helmet stencilled, usually, on the left front bumper together with the standard German tactical sign, indicating the unit's role and number within the division.

The helmet was retained when the division expanded to become the Panzer Corps Grossdeutschland. It remained plain for the Panzer Grenadier Division Grossdeutschland and emblazoned with the Brandenburg eagle for units of the Panzer Grenadier Division Brandenburg. When the Panzer Division Kurmark was raised its tactical sign was the standard white helmet upon which was set the Kurmark eagle. Corps troops wore a steel helmet in yellow as their distinctive mark

Appendix 2
The Organisation of the Infantry Regiment Grossdeutschland as at 1 October 1939

1st Battalion made up of elements drawn from the Wach Regiment. Three rifle companies, a machine-gun company and a heavy weapons company.

2nd Battalion formed from men from 92nd Infantry Regiment. Same composition as 1st Battalion.

3rd Battalion formed from elements of the Infantry Instruction Regiment. Same composition as 1st Battalion.

4th Battalion also formed from the Infantry Instruction Regiment. Was made up of a light infantry gun company, an anti-tank company and a heavy infantry gun company.

In July 1940 a 5th Battalion made up of a motorcycle company, and one each of pioneers, signals and anti-aircraft, was added to the establishment.

Appendix 3
The Organisation of the Infantry Division (Motorised) Grossdeutschland as at 20 June 1942

Two infantry regiments each of three battalions and a heavy weapons battalion. The scale of heavy weapons was particularly high:

1 motorcycle battalion of five companies.
1 tank battalion of three companies (30 Panzer IV) and a flame-thrower battalion 640th assault gun battery which became a battalion with three batteries (21 guns on Panzer 3 chassis). 400th artillery regiment of eleven batteries: 4 light howitzer batteries; 4 heavy howitzer batteries; 1 100mm gun battery; 1 rocket projector battery; 1 observation battery.
1 anti-aircraft battalion of five batteries.
1 anti-tank battalion of three companies.
43rd assault engineer battalion of three companies and one column.
1 signals battalion of two companies and one column,
Divisional services with eighteen lorry columns, three workshop companies, and a medical column.

Appendix 4
Order of Battle, Brandenburg Division as at April 1943

Divisional headquarters: Berlin
1st Regiment: Brandenburg
1st Battalion
2nd Battalion
3rd Battalion
Signals Platoon

2nd Regiment: Admont
1st Battalion
2nd Battalion
3rdBattalion
Signals Platoon

3rd Regiment: Düren near Aachen
1st Battalion
2nd Battalion
3rd Battalion
Signals Platoon

4th Regiment: Brandenburg
1st Battalion
2nd Battalion

Notes: During 1944 a battery of artillery was placed on the establishment of each of the four regiments, and a panzer company to the establishment of 3rd and 4th Regiments during the same year.

Appendix 5
Order of Battle, Panzer Grenadier Division Brandenburg as at January 1945

Divisional headquarters

1st Jäger Regiment
Twelve companies strong:
    Nos 1-3 and 6-8 were Rifle Companies
    Nos 4 and 9 were Heavy Weapons Companies
    Nos 5 and 10 were Mortar Companies
    No. 11 was the Anti-tank Company
    No. 12 was the Pioneer Company

2nd Jäger Regiment
    Composition as for 1st Jäger Regiment

Panzer Group Wietersheim
    An HQ and one battalion of tanks

Assault Artillery Brigade
    An HQ and three batteries of SP guns

Armoured Reconnaissance Battalion
    HQ
    1st Squadron Reconnaissance
    2nd and 3rd Squadrans Armoured Personnel Carrier
    Squadrons
    4th Heavy Squadron

Armoured Artillery Regiment
    HQ
    1st Battalion (Light Howitzer) 3 Batteries
    3rd Battalion (Heavy Howitzer) 1 Battery
    (A 2nd Battalion was not raised)

Armoured Signals Battalion
    An HQ and two compaaies

Assault Engineer Battalion
  An HQ and three companies together with a bridging column.

Army Flak Battalion
  An HQ with two heavy flak batteries and one light flak battery.

Anti-tank Battalion
  HQ
  Nos 1 and 2 Anti-tank Assault Gun Companies
  No. 3 (Motorised) Anti-tank Gun Company

Divisional Ration Column

Motor Transport
  Three companies, a field post office and a workshops company

Horse Drawn Cart Detachment
  An HQ and three squadrons

Medical Detachment

Reinforcenent and Replacement Battalion

Select Bibliography

Awescu, V. and others *Participation of the Romanian Army in the Anti-Hitlerite War.* Military Publishing House, Bucharest, 1966

Arbeitskreis für Wehrforschung *Kriegstagebuch des OKW.* Bernard & Graefe, 1965

Bealer, S. *Stalin and his Generals.* Souvenir Press, 1969

Blaxland, G. *Destination Dunkirk.* Kimber, 1973

Bosch, H. *Der zweite Weltkrieg zwischen Rhein und Maas.* Kreisverwaltung Geldern, 1970

Chaplin, H. *The Queen's Own Royal West Kent Regiment,* 1920-1950. M. Joseph, 1954

Cooper, M. *The German Army, 1939-1945.* Macdonald and Jane's, 1978

Cooper, M. and Lucas, J. *Panzer: The Armoured Force of the Third Reich.* Macdonald and Jane's, 1976

Erikson, J. *The Road to Stalingrad.* Weidenfeld & Nicolson, 1975

Esposito, J. *A Military History of World War Two.* US Military Academy, 1953

Fillies, F. *Grossdeutschland Grenadiere Zeitgeschichte.* Verlag, 1941

Froben, H.J. *Aufklärende Artillerie.* Schild Verlag, 1970

Garthof, F.L. *Die Sowjet Armee: Wesen und Lehre.* Markus Verlag, 1953

Guderian, H. *Mit den Panzer im Ost und West.* Volk U Reich Verlag

Haupt, W. *Heeresgruppe Mitte.* Podzun, 1968

Hermann, C.H. *68 Kriegsmonate: Die 9te Panzer Division im 2ten Weltkrieg.* Kameradschaft der Division, Wien, 1975

Keilig *Das Heer* (Three volumes). Henniag Verlag

Klein, E. und Kuhn *Tiger: Die Geschichte einer legendaren Waffe, 1942-45.* Motorbuch Verlag, 1976

Kurowski and Tornau *Sturmartillerie.* Maximilian Verlag

Macksey, K. *Guderian: Panzer General.* Macdonald and Jane's, 1975

Mellenthin, F.W. von *Panzerschlachten 1939-45.* Vowinkel Verlag, 1962

Michels, W. *Niaderrheinisches Land im Krieg.* Boss Druck, 1964

Middeldorf, E. *Taktik im Russlandfeldzug.* Mittler, 1956

Munzel, O. *Die Deutschen Gepanzerten Truppen.* Maximilian Verlag

O'Ballance, E. *The Red Army.* Faber, 1964

Parotkin, and others *Kurskaya Bitva.* Progress Publishers, Moscow, 1974

Piekalkiewicz, J. *Fieseler Fi 156 Storch im zweiten Weltkrieg.* Motorbuch Verlag, 1977

Piekalkiewicz, J. *Stalingrad: Anatomie einer Schlacht.* Süd-westverlag, 1977

Sebger u Etterlin *Die 24 Panzer Division, 1939-45.* Vowinkel Verlag, 1962

Shilovski, E. *Rozgrom Nemetskikh Voisk v Byelo-Rossiyi.* Unpublished manuscript

Simon, Max *Soviet Russian Infantry and Armoured Forces.* Unpublished manuscript

Stoves *1 Panzer Division, 1935-1945.* Podzun Verlag, 1964

Tessing, G. *Ubersicht von Truppen der Deutsch Wehrmacht und Waffen SS, 1939-45.* Biblios Verlag, 1977

. US Army *Combat in Russian Forests and Swamps*. Department of the Army
US Army *Effects of Climate on Combat Conditions in European Russia*. Department of the Army
US Army *Terrain Factors in the Russian Campaign*. Department of the Army
Weidinger, O. *Das Reich Division*. Munin Verlag, 1973
Die Geschichte des Panzerkorps Grossdeutschland (three volumes) Traditionsverlag
Weltkrieg 1939-45: Ehrenbuch der Deutschen Wehrmacht Geschichte der 3 Panzer Division
Istoriya Velikoi Otechesvennoi Sovyetskovo Soyussa. Moscow, 1961/64
Various other regimental accounts, war diaries, personal diaries and interviews.